Praise for
Rock-Solid Kids

During those beginning years of the Awana ministry, over 50 years ago, I often prayed, "Lord! Send us gifted people who have a passion and a heartbeat to reach kids with the Gospel." Larry Fowler, the author of *Rock-Solid Kids*, is the one God has raised up in these challenging days to arouse Christian leadership to rescue young people and teach them God's Word while they are reachable. God has blessed our author with unusual teaching abilities. I urge you to read and use this book to challenge your church leadership to support this urgent vision.

Art Rorheim
Cofounder/President Emeritus
Awana Clubs International

For over 25 years, Larry Fowler has been teaching all over the world about what the Bible says in regard to children's ministry. This outstanding book is rock-solid and has biblically centered material that will impact every parent and children's ministry leader. This material, if read with an open heart and mind, moves us to ask the question, "What does God's Word clearly say about children's and family ministries?" This is a must-read for all of us who love and obey God's Word.

J. Michael Broyles, D.R.E.
Educational Pastor
Grace Baptist Church
Santa Clarita, CA

I finished reading *Rock-Solid Kids*. I must say it was hard to put down. I read it in a few hours and find myself pouring over it time and again. You have done a marvelous job, squarely hitting the nail on the head. I found the book to be refreshingly candid, biblically accurate, hard-hitting and truthful. In 20 years of ministry to children, I've not found a better book that lays out the state, need and importance of children's ministry. *Rock-Solid Kids* is a must-read for all parents, pastors and those serving in leadership with children.

Thanks again for writing a marvelous book that I believe will have an impact on children's ministry for decades to come.

Jerry Easley
Minister to Preschool and Children
First Baptist Church Ocala
Ocala, Florida

Children need a foundation for life. The psalmist cried, "If the foundations are destroyed, what can the righteous do?" All of society bears the injury and shares the cost of faulty foundations. This book provides a blueprint for churches and families to build strong and secure foundations for the future. It is simple in style yet filled with insight and instruction that will help you and your church build with confidence. I highly recommend it.

Dr. Jack Graham

Pastor
Prestonwood Baptist Church
Plano, Texas

Rock-Solid Kids is exactly that—rock solid! This is the finest book I have ever seen on children's ministry. I wholeheartedly recommend it. It is entirely practical, especially helpful and thoroughly biblical. Get one for yourself and several for your children's workers.

Dr. Jerry Falwell

Founder and Chancellor
Liberty University
Lynchburg, Virginia

Rock-Solid Kids should become a primer in the area of children's ministry. It has the right foundation—the Word of God, the right relevance—changing the lives of kids and their families, and the right application—this IS our golden hour for reaching kids for Christ.

Rock-Solid Kids should become a best-seller. It is a must for all children's ministers, workers and parents. I would challenge pastors to read this book and get energized about making a difference in the lives of kids. Children are not just the church of the future—they are our hope for the present.

Rock-Solid Kids struck a responsive chord with me. I have met Larry Fowler and believe in what he is doing to touch the lives of kids for Christ. This book is foundational to an effective children's ministry.

Dr. Edward Johnson

Pastor
First Baptist Church
Ocala, Florida

Larry Fowler is a seasoned veteran who challenges parents and church leaders to put children at the center of our concern. He leads us into the Word of God and shows convincingly why this is true, and how it can be done. As the father of five adult children, I can affirm that *Rock-Solid Kids* is on target in addressing a pressing need the church must face.

Dr. Norm Wakefield

Phoenix Seminary, Arizona

Rock-Solid
KIDS

Larry Fowler

Gospel Light

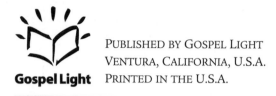

PUBLISHED BY GOSPEL LIGHT
VENTURA, CALIFORNIA, U.S.A.
PRINTED IN THE U.S.A.

Gospel Light

Gospel Light is a Christian publisher dedicated to serving the local church. We believe God's vision for Gospel Light is to provide church leaders with biblical, user-friendly materials that will help them evangelize, disciple and minister to children, youth and families.

It is our prayer that this Gospel Light book will help you discover biblical truth for your own life and help you meet the needs of others. May God richly bless you.

For a free catalog of resources from Gospel Light, please call your Christian supplier or contact us at 1-800-4-GOSPEL *or* www.gospellight.com.

Written by Larry Fowler, Executive Director of Program and Training, Awana Clubs International.

Cover and interior design by Rob Williams

Library of Congress Cataloging-in-Publication Data

Fowler, Larry.
  Rock-solid kids : giving children a biblical foundation for life / Larry Fowler.
    p. cm.
  Includes bibliographical references and index.
  ISBN 0-8307-3713-8 (hard) -- ISBN 0-8307-3732-4 (trade pbk.)
  1. Church work with children. I. Title.
  BV639.C4F69 2005
  259'.22--dc22   2004024744

    4 5 6 7 8 9 10 11 12 13 14 15 16 / 14 13 12 11 10 09 08 07 06 05

Contents

Foreword

There has never been a time in history when the children of the world have been more spiritually at risk than they are today. Society has never had so many inroads to indoctrinate the hearts of children as they have today. Only a generation ago, ultraviolent video games, the Internet and the overt child-targeted efforts of Hollywood, Madison Avenue and the publishing world were simply unimaginable to most of us.

And society has never provided so much corruption for consumption by the masses as it does today. A plethora of competing worldviews and warped values flow freely throughout society—directly into the minds of children, where they stay for a lifetime.

Where are the parents? Trying to stay afloat amidst crazed, hectic schedules that allow little time for meaningful spiritual interaction with their children. Childhood itself is compressed as kids are forced into the same stressful lifestyles as their parents. Who has time today to "be still and know that I am God?"

Where is the church? How is it faring in this battle for the hearts and minds of children? Not terribly well at all, I'm afraid. For that rare church that even recognizes that the stakes have risen dramatically in the last several years, they are for the most part attempting to fight off twenty-first-century monsters with nineteenth-century weapons.

Together, parents and churches have settled into a destructive co-dependent relationship. Parents, with little inclination and few high-quality resources to devote to the spiritual nurture of their children, have largely abdicated the job to the church. And the church has readily taken on a task that was originally mandated in Scripture to the parents of children. Where Scripture is clear that the primary role in raising spiritual children belongs to the parents, with the church in a supporting role, we find today that this biblical model is flipped upside-down. How can God honor something so contrary to His Word?

Does all of this lead you to believe that you are reading the words of a defeatist? Not at all! Be assured that I am an optimist—in the Lord. God has made it clear in His Word that He will honor the efforts of those who do things His way—and that includes parents and churches. I believe that a proper, biblical working relationship between parents and the local church will unleash God's blessings and spark a revolution in children's ministry—and save a generation from spiritual bankruptcy.

Within this book that you are holding, my good friend Larry Fowler has taken us back to the source—the Word of God—to help us regain our bearing as it pertains to raising a generation of spiritual champions. It is a book that is long overdue.

Please read this book carefully and prayerfully. Ask God to show you what place He has for you in what may well be the greatest rescue mission of our day—snatching our children from the grip of a society that wants nothing less than their minds, bodies, hearts and souls. Let us first rise up and declare that those things belong to the God of the ages, and then let us fall to our knees to seek His way to reclaim them in His name.

Jack Eggar
President/CEO
Awana Clubs International
November 2004

Introduction

*Therefore everyone who hears these words of mine and puts them into
practice is like a wise man who built his house on the rock.*

MATTHEW 7:24, *NIV*

Jesus' parable about the men who built their homes on two different foundations inspired the old children's classic song that begins like this:

The wise man built his house upon the rock,
The wise man built his house upon the rock,
The wise man built his house upon the rock,
And the house on the rock stood firm.

Remember the fate of the foolish man's house later in the song?

And the house on the sand went splat!

The point? If your life is going to stand, then you've got to build it on the right foundation—and that's the Word of God! Jesus is the rock in other passages. *But in this parable, the rock is the Word of God.*

Those involved in children's ministry must also build on the right foundation—and that is the primary concern of this book. For decades, children across North America sang "the wise man built his house upon the rock" and then "the foolish man built his house upon the sand." Yet children's ministry itself has begun to look more and more like the foolish man—ignoring the importance of a firm foundation of biblical content.

Children's ministry is being pushed and pulled by educational models, statistical analysis, growth techniques, cultural change and technological advancements. But with the weight of all these influences, little attention is given to what ought to be the most important influence in molding the shape of children's ministry—*the Word of God.* All of these other influences can be very helpful, but they should build upon scriptural truths, not the other way around.

So what does the Bible have to say about what children's ministry should look like? Children's ministry as a distinct part of the local church appears nowhere in Scripture. There is no mention of Sunday School, VBS, or any other children's program. Yet, God's Word has much to say about kids. Many passages refer to children, speak of ministering to children and give directions or promises to children. Among these many passages about children are some that clearly can help us mold our ministry to them.

Do you immediately picture church when you hear children's ministry? I confess—I do, too often. But children's ministry takes place in the home as well as in the church. In fact, you will find that the home is the *primary* place that ministry to children must occur.

Whether your children's ministry is in your home or in your church, the purpose of this book is to enable you to build a children's ministry that is rock solid—*modeled upon scriptural teaching:*

- Each chapter of this book starts with a Scripture passage—a "rock" for your foundation.
- The Scripture passage *specifically* refers to children or ministering to them.
- Each chapter contains a thorough discussion of implications and applications.
- Together, the eight core chapters will give you eight "foundation rocks"—fundamental principles from God's Word upon which to build your ministry.

Few of us get the luxury of starting something from scratch—the way we want to. For many, this book will mean propping up the house while the foundation is built under it. But the foundation must be there—or our spiritual house will go splat!

Here's the challenge: *Can your church or your home have a rock-solid ministry to children—a Bible-solid children's ministry? Is the right foundation in place?*

This book will guide you. It will focus your attention on the rock of God's Word as the place to start in deciding how to build your children's ministry.

CHAPTER 1

Not a Pretty Picture

The Importance of Children's Ministry

But when Jesus saw it, He was greatly displeased.

MARK 10:14

You've seen the picture often titled "Jesus Blesses the Children." It is a popular scene for artists to depict. Usually, the children and Jesus are shown interacting happily with butterflies flitting by. The grass and trees look like they are straight out of the Garden of Eden. It is serene. Jesus is happy. And, if a picture is only meant to show Mark 10:16, it may very well be pretty accurate. But then, there is the rest of the story . . .

The Context

Mark 10:1-2 says,

> He arose from there and came to the region of Judea by the other side of the Jordan. And multitudes gathered to Him again, and as He was accustomed, He taught them again. The Pharisees came and asked Him, "Is it lawful for a man to divorce his wife?" testing Him.

In verses 1-9, the Pharisees were debating Jesus. As they had done before, they were trying to trip Him up. They were testing Him. The issue of divorce was a hot topic, something about which there was quite a bit of disagreement in Jesus' day. The Pharisees wanted to try to draw Him into that current controversy. Jesus' answers to them were very wise, and He startled them with His answers, as He usually did.

The setting changed in verse 10 from a public one to a private home: "In the house His disciples also asked Him again about the same matter." Probably, the Pharisees had left, though the passage doesn't say for sure. "In the house" implies that Jesus and His disciples retired to a more private setting—not completely private—but at least they were back together as a group. The disciples probably wanted to understand His answer more thoroughly, so they had some further questions. They asked Jesus to give them more information about the topic of divorce, and in verses 11 and 12, He explained it more.

The Disciples' Error

In the middle of this discussion—we're not told that it ends—there was an interruption. This conversation in which the disciples had a great deal of interest was suddenly disrupted by the arrival of parents bringing their young children so that Jesus would bless them (verse 13):

> Then they brought little children to Him, that He might touch them; but the disciples rebuked those who brought them.

The children who were brought to Jesus were likely infants or young toddlers. Some scholars believe that it was a tradition to bring children at one year of age to a rabbi in a synagogue for his blessing. And so, it could very well have been that these children were brought to Jesus for His blessing and His prayer for them. Scripture says, "They brought young children to him, that he might touch them" (verse 13).

In the second part of verse 13, the scene switches from focusing on the parents to focusing on the disciples: "The disciples rebuked those who brought them." The *disciples* rebuked the *parents*.

Why do you think the disciples rebuked the parents? What was the underlying attitude of the disciples that caused them to rebuke the parents? The disciples were busy learning, and so they probably thought, *This just isn't the time.* They didn't appreciate the disruption.

Note the sequence of action: Parents bring young children; the disciples become upset; the disciples rebuke the parents.

Jesus' Reaction

Since Jesus' emotional reaction is only recorded in Mark (parallel passages are Matthew 19:13-15 and Luke 18:15-17), it often gets overlooked. An artist who paints this scene without studying the Mark account will portray a happy, peaceful occasion.

However, we can't appreciate the full impact of the passage, nor understand it accurately, without noting how Jesus responded in verse 14:

But when Jesus saw it, He was greatly displeased and said to them, "Let the little children come to Me, and do not forbid them; for of such is the kingdom of God."

The other two accounts don't say He was displeased. When we read the Matthew and Luke accounts, we might imagine Jesus speaking in very nice, gentle, pearly tones, saying, "Let the children come." It just sounds so wonderful—so majestic.

But Mark tells us it didn't happen that way at all! Jesus' emotional response is revealed in verse 14. We see how He reacted, and wow, was He angry! He was greatly displeased! It was definitely a strong, negative emotional reaction. In fact, if you compare Scripture, you'll find that it was a very, very strong reaction in light of the other emotional reactions that Jesus had.

But *why* was He angry? Would Jesus have become angry by accident? Or was His anger purposeful?

And what was He angry at? What made Him displeased?

Clearly, Jesus had a point to make. And clearly, it was the actions and the attitude of the disciples that were the focus of His anger. It was the way they rebuked the parents for bringing the children. Let's clarify this picture: The disciples were upset at the parents; Jesus became upset at the disciples. The parents thought they were doing something good. They *were*. The disciples should have been pleased. They *weren't!* The disciples thought *they* were doing something good. They *weren't*. They thought Jesus would be pleased with them. He *wasn't!*

What did the disciples do that made Jesus so angry? Consider their thinking: They thought children were an interruption. They thought blessing children was less important than the discussion they were having. That attitude was the basis for their actions and was the reason for Jesus' anger. To put it another way, they thought adult issues were more important than ministering to children.

Jesus' reaction was extremely strong. In fact, there is only one other place in Scripture where Jesus is this angry—His reaction to the moneychangers in the Temple (see Luke 19:45-48). Jesus was angry because the disciples put a higher priority on discussing an adult topic than on ministering to children. The disciples simply didn't see children as they should have seen children.

Our View of Children

In local churches and families, four different attitudes toward children are seen.

Attitude 1: Children Are a Bother.
This view is wrong!

You know the attitude—we *have* to take care of them, especially during the worship service! There *has* to be a children's church, because the children will distract the attention of the adults! We *have* to do *something* with them—even if it is just showing them a video to keep them quiet. Somebody's got to do it or else ministry to adults will be hindered. Possibly, the disciples themselves would have had this attitude.

When this attitude is present, there is apathy toward children's ministry.

When this thinking infiltrates the church, it reveals itself through the alignment of resources. The best of recruiting efforts, church budgets, facility upkeep, etc., are reserved for adult ministry and children's ministry gets the leftovers.

But children's workers can also have this attitude: Lesson preparation is at a bare minimum; little attention is given to learning objectives; there is no communication or cooperation with the children's parents; and the various children's ministries do not coordinate their efforts.

When this thinking is in the home, the television becomes the primary tool to keep the kids quiet. Parents secretly are glad when their children play video games, because they are not bothered. Rarely do they give the spiritual nurture of their children a thought. It's never a priority.

Attitude 2: Children Are a Tool.
This view is practical!

Without a doubt, this view is common in Western churches. Children *are* potential tools for reaching their families. Pastors and church leaders who focus on church growth understand that one of the most effective ways to build a church is to have an effective children's ministry. And so the value given to children's ministry is due to its potential for reaching adults. Such a view is inadequate. It's good—and it works—but it's inadequate.

When this attitude is present, there is approval of children's ministry. In comparison with the first attitude, children's ministry has more value to church leadership.

In the church, children's workers are lauded. But the leaders' interest is in how many parents are brought in through the children's ministry. All of the activities and programs of the children's department are assessed in light of the impact upon the adult population of the church.

Pathetically, parents often use children as tools, too. A Little League dad may try to find fulfillment of his own dreams in his son. A divorced mom may manipulate the activities or emotions of a child to get even with her ex-husband.

Attitude 3: Children Are Our Future.

This view is true!

On several occasions Moses reminded the children of Israel of this view of children (see Deuteronomy 4:40; 6:1-2). And nothing has changed since—we understand that if we don't minister to children, Christianity will die. They are the instruments of carrying the message of the gospel to another generation and into the future. We see how important all of that is. Such a view is essential—but it also is inadequate. This view still sees children as a tool to accomplish another end.

When this attitude is present, there is appreciation of children's ministry. It receives attention. Workers are recognized and adequate facilities and curricula are a concern.

Vladimir Belous was a pastor in Ukraine during the years of Soviet rule. He learned of the importance of children's ministry from communist propaganda. One day, he saw a flyer that essentially said, "The real danger from America is not their missiles, but that they are teaching their children about God." The pamphlet went on to describe (in a very derogatory manner) the efforts in the United States churches to train their children, and to warn the people of the Soviet Union not to allow such contamination in their country, or the future of communism would be in doubt. Pastor Belous knew at once that children's ministry was essential to his church if it was to survive into the future. Out of this conviction came an openness to establish children's ministry, and his church became the beachhead for launching the Awana Club ministry in Ukraine.

Attitude 4: Children Are People.

This view is the best—because it is biblical and because it is Jesus' view.

Close your eyes and say the word "people." What do you see? Only adults? Or are there children in your mind's picture? When the disciples saw the little children who were brought to Jesus, they didn't see people. Maybe they saw future people, but not real-time people.

Jesus' response demonstrates a different perspective. He *didn't* say to the disciples, "Let the little children come to Me, because they are our future;" rather, He scolded them, "Let the little children come to me, . . . for the kingdom of God belongs to such as these" (Mark 10:14, *NIV*). In other words, not merely because of their *future* value, but because of their *present* value—the little children were important to Jesus. They were real-time people who needed Him. To Jesus, a child was definitely not a bother, not merely a tool, not someone with future value, but a real person—now. He stopped what He was doing and gave the children His full attention.

When we see children as Jesus sees them, ministering to them becomes a priority:

- In the church, children's ministry takes its place on equal footing with other ministries. The budget reflects the equal value of children's ministry. Church objectives include the equal importance of children's ministry. Facility use demonstrates the equal significance of children's ministry. Its leadership is on "peer status" with other ministry leaders.
- Parents demonstrate their conviction that the most important training they can provide for their children is spiritual training.

They, like Jesus, are willing to spend time in the spiritual nurture of their children.

Which attitude is prevalent in your church? If you are a parent, which attitude best describes your regular pattern of activity? As a children's worker, does your preparation time reflect the best attitude?
Think through this summary. Which perspective is yours?

Figure 1

	Children Are	Attitude	There Is
1	A bother	Wrong	Apathy
2	A tool	Practical	Approval
3	Our future	True	Appreciation
4	People	Biblical	A priority

Jesus' Response

One thing is very clear: Children were important to Jesus.

When He said "Let the little children come," He didn't do it in a peaceful scene. He didn't do it outside in a beautiful, green parklike setting. He didn't do it with gentle tones and a peaceful look on His face. Instead, the words "Let the little children come" were words of strong anger. When Jesus spoke them, the message was sharp and full of emotion! It was a strong rebuke to the disciples for their actions. This scene was not at all the way that it is usually painted.

My Testimony

At age 13, I committed my life to working with children at a Bible camp. God has graciously allowed me to participate in children's ministry ever since. Yet there have been many occasions when I have sensed from others the attitude, *When are you going to get a real ministry?* The most important attitude of all, however, is that of my Savior. And if *He* thinks ministry to children is important, that's all I need!

"He was indignant" (Mark 10:14, *NIV*). Three words that reveal so very much! They make one issue really clear: Jesus saw children as worthy of His time. To Him, they were a priority.

Foundation Rock 1: Ministering to children is a high priority.

Ministry to children too often gets pushed down, shoved aside, put off. It gets treated as second-rate, receives secondhand resources and is expected to play second fiddle to "real" ministry—adult ministry.

But not by Jesus. He demonstrated that it was very important.

And if children's ministry is important to Jesus, that's all I need.

Resources

Barna, George. *Transforming Children into Spiritual Champions.* Ventura, CA: Regal Books, 2003.
This dynamic book is one of a kind. It provides compelling statistical evidence and persuasive thoughts regarding the need to make children's ministry a priority in the church.

Gospel Light. *Children's Ministry Smart Pages.* Ventura, CA: Gospel Light, 2004.
This book provides children's ministry leaders with up-to-date guidelines and tools for creating and carrying out a vision for ministering to children.

Haystead, Wes and Sheryl. *Children's Ministry:*
No Higher Calling. **Ventura, CA: Gospel Light, 1998.**
This video will inspire you to embrace the important role of teaching children of all ages about God's Word and His amazing love.

Haystead, Wes and Sheryl. *How to Have a Great Sunday School.*
Ventura, CA: Gospel Light, 2000.
A must-have resource that gives expert advice and proven methods to help both small and large churches plan and organize their Sunday Schools for effective Bible teaching.

London, H. B., Jr., and Neil B. Wiseman. *For Kids' Sake: Winning the*
Tug-of-War for Future Generations. **Ventura, CA: Regal Books, 2004.**
This book will instruct you about the critical importance of instilling a biblical worldview in children.

CHAPTER 2

Give It Back!

The Responsibility for Children's Ministry

And, fathers, do not provoke your children to anger; but bring them up in the discipline and instruction of the Lord.

EPHESIANS 6:4, *NASB*

The gathering lasted three hours. *Three* sermons. Men sat on one side of the church, women on the other. All the children were seated in the balcony. Latecomers stood in the aisle the entire time. Communion was observed with a common cup with real wine. All the music sounded mournful. No smiles. The call to repentance took 45 minutes.

For a Westerner with experience only in western evangelical churches, the Russian church service in Kazakhstan was certainly eye opening.

As a special guest and one of the preachers, I sat on the stage behind the pulpit, facing the audience. I especially noticed the children in the balcony—they were all ages, from four or five years old up through the teens. Their parents weren't with them; only a few adults were scattered among the children. They amazed me—they sat still for the whole three hours! I thought of what American children would do, and I wondered how the Russians did it.

But why did the children attend the entire service? Later, I asked my Russian hosts, "Don't you have a Sunday School for the children?" Their blank look revealed that they didn't understand my concern. "The parents teach them" was their simple explanation.

I thought this answer was weird. They didn't seem to want a children's Sunday School. They didn't seem to *need* a children's Sunday School. And my team and I were there to present Awana, a midweek children's ministry, to them? How could we get them to start Awana when they didn't even see the need for a Sunday School?

That church, and others in Kazakhstan, have now used the Awana club ministry for 10 years. But they have used it to evangelize the unsaved, not to disciple their own children. And if you ask them why, they will tell you that they don't need it, that the parents teach the children.

Strange, huh? Or is it?

If we are to develop a biblically based children's ministry, the first question we should ask is, "Whose job is it?" Who should own the ministry? Who *is* responsible to train the children?

The Bible is clear.

Parents.

Not children's workers in the church.

Parents.

Not children's organizations or children's publishers.

Parents.

Not Christian schools.

Parents.

The answer is simple, but the implications are challenging and enormous. In fact, this simple truth, by itself, has a Richter-scale impact on current trends and practices in the home and in children's ministry.

Parents have given the responsibility for spiritual training to children's workers. If we are going to build a rock-solid, biblical model, then we must give the responsibility back!

Research consistently affirms the declining biblical worldview (a perspective of life grounded in biblical truth) of our young people. It is nothing short of a crisis, even among committed Christian families! What will stop it? There is very little anyone can do, unless the home (and hence the parents) are involved at the core.[1]

A determined attempt to implement this one simple truth will reverse the trend. It will energize the home around something other than television, Internet, video games and sports. It will also revolutionize Sunday School and midweek club ministries. It will impact the nursery. It will force changes in youth ministries. It will revise curricula. It will not eliminate children's ministry (like the Kazakhstan church), but it will revolutionize it.

I have always believed every church should have a children's ministry. I've personally invested my life in Awana—a children's ministry for local churches. But I have discovered that there is no scriptural reference to children in the church apart from their parents (someone will no doubt mention the incident described in Acts 20:9 in which Eutychus fell out of the window when Paul preached too long).

What then is the church to do? If parents have the responsibility, what are children's workers to do? Do they have a role?

Before we think about the answers to these questions, let's examine the scriptural principles. Consider these truths from the Old Testament:

Genesis 18:19 (*NIV*)—"For I have chosen [Abraham], so that he will direct his children and his household after him to keep the way of the LORD."

Deuteronomy 4:10 (*NIV*)—"Assemble the people before me to hear my words so that they . . . may teach them to their children."

Deuteronomy 6:6-7—"These words which I command you today shall be in your heart. You shall teach them diligently to your children."

Deuteronomy 32:46 (*NIV*)—"Command your children to obey carefully all the words of this law."

Joshua 24:15—"As for me and my house, we will serve the LORD."

Psalm 78:5-6 (*NIV*)—"He commanded our forefathers to teach their children, so the next generation would know them, . . . and they in turn would tell their children."

These verses make the mandate clear: Parents have the responsibility— and privilege—to plant and nurture faith in their children.

Understanding Ephesians 6:4

In just 18 words, this verse clearly focuses the issue. It has four phrases that guide us specifically in developing ministry to children. We will look at these phrases in this chapter.

1. *"Fathers"*
This tells us who *owns* the responsibility.

I've already said that a biblical approach to children's ministry begins with the answer to the question, Who is responsible to train the children?

If you ask God, He will tell you. The answer is simple—parents. But wait—doesn't the verse say "fathers"? Are mothers off the hook?

No—the context demands they be included. In Ephesians 6:1, children are commanded to obey their *parents*. In Ephesians, Paul addresses three pairs of relationships. Each is reciprocal—in other words, the advice has to do with relationships described by a line with arrows at either end:

Wives ⇔ Husbands (5:22,25)

Children ⇔ Parents (6:1,4)

Servants ⇔ Masters (6:5,9)

In context, verse 4 includes moms, rather than dads only, making it consistent with verse 1.

No—other Scriptures emphasize the role of the mother, as in 2 Timothy 1:5, in which Timothy's mother and grandmother are recognized for their role in developing Timothy's faith.

But why did God inspire the apostle Paul to use the word for fathers? Maybe because dads are more prone than moms to shun this responsibility? All too often the moms alone shoulder the burden for the spiritual upbringing of children—even in committed Christian two-parent households. While mothers certainly are not excluded, fathers are *definitely included!*

Dads, you can't escape it. This verse is for *you!* Your active involvement in spiritual training is needed. What could we predict about the future of a child whose father says he is a believer but is only marginally involved in leading the spiritual development of the family? Those who study families generally agree that a highly influential factor in a child's life is how important spiritual training is to his or her father! Maybe that's why God had Paul use the word for fathers.

If you don't feel equipped for spiritual teaching, you can't just give up or admit defeat! Spiritual teaching is too critical. You can find tools; you will get some later in this book. You *can* do it!

Not only are too many Christian homes lacking the father's involvement in spiritual teaching, but children's ministries need support from fathers as well. When fathers are involved in Sunday School, Awana or other children's ministries, they become more aware of the need to be role models at home, and they also provide a male spiritual influence in the lives of children who lack one.[2]

2. "Do Not Provoke Your Children to Anger"

Do you know any children provoked to anger by their fathers? We will discuss this phrase in chapter 5.

3. "Bring Them Up"

Active—not passive—that's the sense here. If this verse were in the passive voice, it would be translated "have them brought up" or "make sure they are brought up." Parents are not to *delegate* this responsibility but to *do* it. This is not an educational decision. It is a lifestyle decision for parents.

Yet, too many Christian parents have abrogated their responsibility, relying on children's ministries in the local church and Christian schools to do what is first their work. And too many children's ministries and Christian schools have accepted that responsibility with open arms. We've done it in Awana. It is not meant to be a drop-off ministry, giving mom and dad a free babysitting night, but it is used that way. Churches and Christian schools need to find effective ways to engage parents and draw them back to their biblical role.

Who's Responsible?

Any mom or dad who is a believer would quickly agree that he or she is responsible for spiritually training his or her own children. But how we interpret what being responsible means is producing some serious, unwanted results in some Christian homes and churches all throughout our Western culture.

If you follow the flow of this wrong thinking, you will see some really bad results.

1. What parents think:
    a. They understand that they are responsible.
    b. They perceive children's workers in the church as experts in training children spiritually.

2. What parents feel:
    a. They feel inadequate themselves.
    b. They feel children's workers are adequate.
3. Consequently, what parents do:
    a. They send their children to Sunday School, children's church, Awana, other weekday clubs or Christian Schools.
    b. They are grateful to their church for teaching their children.

None of this is bad. But what follows can be devastating.

1. What parents conclude:
    a. They then feel they have fulfilled their responsibility for spiritual training, because it is being done at church.
    b. Since they think it is being done at church, they do little reinforcement at home.

2. What consequences result:
    a. Spiritual training then becomes another activity in the child's life, rather than an integral part of life.
    b. The child doesn't observe or experience a link between the spiritual training and everyday activities.
    c. The child doesn't adopt the spiritual training into his or her worldview.

The local church, and its children's workers, can help parents realize that being passively involved in their child's spiritual growth is not acceptable.

So far, Ephesians 6:4 has told us two things:

1. Who owns the responsibility? Primarily, the parents.
2. Who performs the responsibility? Primarily, the parents.

There is one more thought: What does the responsibility include?

4. "In the Discipline and Instruction of the Lord."

Picture beautiful grounds surrounding an equally beautiful home. The grounds cover many acres. They are full of healthy fruit trees; there are many gardens and other things for children to enjoy, and the grounds are entirely safe. Around the grounds is a large wall. Suppose you inherit the home, and as you show it to your children for the first time, you say to them, "This is where you are going to grow up—within these boundaries." That is what "in" means—within the boundaries of.

Parents are to bring their children up within the boundaries, or the walls, that the training and instruction of the Lord provides. It is safe. It is healthy. It is a beautiful, wonderful place for children to grow up!

But what *is* training and instruction? You will learn specifically what this means in chapter 4.

Giving the Responsibility Back

I can hear the objections:

- From a children's pastor—"Our parents don't know how to train their children!"
- From a parent—"Our family is so busy, there just isn't time!"
- From a children's worker—"The parents are happy to just leave their kids with us; they don't seem interested!"

But God would not give us a command that is impossible. We *can* get the responsibility aligned properly—and here's how to do it.

When Parents Are Unaware or Unprepared

This is the most common situation. In this case, the *church leadership* needs to act. Ministry to children and ministry to adults must be integrated so that parents learn how to fulfill their role as spiritual teachers. When integration is effective, parents discover effective tools to use.

Picture this after-church car conversation:

"Michael, what was your Sunday School lesson about today?"

"Jonah."

"That's good," his mom replies. "Ours was about Jesus' sermon on the mount."

And Michael and his Mom move on to other subjects.

No connection. Limited conversation. Without integrating content, parents are less equipped to follow up on what their children are taught in children's ministry.

In this case, churches minister *to* the parents and *to* the children. There is *no connection* between the two, either in purpose or content. Separateness is emphasized, rather than integration. It looks like this:

Figure 2

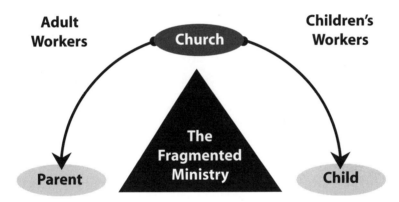

Certainly, the church needs to minister to both parents and children. Ephesians 4:12-13 commands the church to prepare people for works of service, and if children are saved, they are certainly included. Yet the disconnection does not serve to encourage the biblical model of parent responsibility.

One message on the subject every year won't do it—though that's a great start. There must be a continuous effort to raise awareness and train parents.

Here are some approaches that churches have found helpful:

- Include sermon discussion points for the family every Sunday in the bulletin, encouraging parents to use them on the way home.
- Keep parents aware of what their children are learning in Sunday School or other children's programs—even provide them with a curriculum overview. The overview is presented as "this is what you will want to reinforce in your child," not "this is what we are teaching your child" (get the difference?).
- As a last item in adult Bible classes, group parents together for five minutes to discuss the question, What can we share with our children from this lesson?
- Periodically, coordinate the curriculum in a parents' Bible class with their children's curriculum.
- Regularly invite parents to share how their families have benefited from the parents' involvement in spiritual training. Print articles in church newsletters or post them on church websites, or briefly interview parents during adult classes or worship services.

When Parents Are Unsaved or Unwilling

There is much that children's workers can do to reach parents and equip them to fulfill their role.

How about this car conversation?

"Michael, did you have fun in church today?"

"Yeah. Mom, my teacher said I should tell you the story I heard. Can I?"

Directed conversation. Initiated by the teacher. Performed by the child. What a tool! But it means that the teacher will not see the child's understanding of a Bible truth as the end of the process—that is not completed until the parent has heard as well!

In this model, the church ministers *to* the child and then *through* the child *to* the parent.

Figure 3

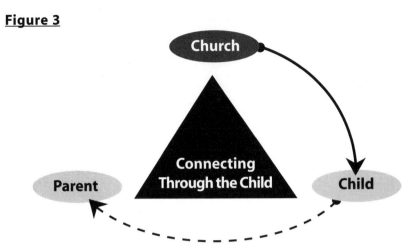

Children's workers can do these things:

- E-mail the parents regularly, including a request to ask their children, "What was one thing you did in class today? What happened in the Bible story you heard?" Parents of older children can be encouraged to ask, "What is something you learned God wants you to do? What did you learn about what God is like?" Include a message for parents to share with their children.
- Phone the parents. When you phone, *praise* their children! You can build a relationship with parents fast when they know you like their children! Don't know what to say? Mention something positive about the children's behavior or attitude if you can. If that would take stretching the truth, mention something positive about a child's appearance ("I loved Joel's shirt Sunday"), energy or sociability—*find something!*
- Talk to the parents when they pick up their children. Tell the parents something specific their children did or said ("Riley was really helpful to a visitor today" "Kayley had great ideas in our discussion time").
- Invite parents into the classroom either for the whole session or just for the last few minutes so that they hear the end of the lesson. Then you can suggest: "Kids, ask your parents about

this later today or sometime this week."
- Have celebratory events. Invite the parents. Get the support of key church parents to help you build relationships with the others.
- Have a sign-in table with greeters. Wherever parents drop off their children, *make* a reason for the parents to talk to the greeter.

All of these have a purpose: to build relationships with parents, first to share the gospel and then to involve parents in the spiritual guidance of their children.

When Parents Are Saved and Willing.

Mom and dad, does that description fit you? Once you understand that the responsibility for the spiritual training of your children is yours, here's what you can do:

Take what you are learning, and look for ways to transmit it to your children. How about beginning the car conversation like this? "Michael, I think your Sunday School class was about Jonah today, wasn't it? In our class, we were also learning about obeying God, but we were studying Nehemiah. What do you remember about Nehemiah?"

See, parents lead in the spiritual teaching of their children. The church equips the parents. Children's workers assist the parents. Children get a double dose. Here's the model:

Figure 4

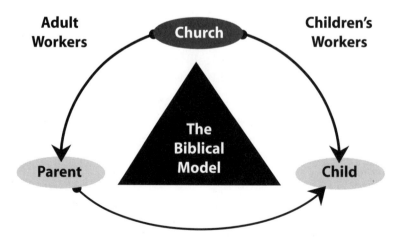

Look right? Here's what parents can do.

First, adopt these perspectives:

- The spiritual training of your children is the most important part of their education—and something that will have limited impact if you don't lead it!
- Children's workers in the church assist you with your responsibility, not the other way around.
- The instruction you receive from your church is valuable information to pass on to your children. They may not be ready to process everything you have learned, but sharing what God's Word means to you will build interest in the child.

Then, follow it with action.

- Spend time in teaching your children (more on this in chapter 3). Make it regular, and follow a plan. In other words, use a family devotional guide or other curriculum.
- Regularly communicate these four points to your children (you'll think of many more, I'm sure, but these are a start).
    1. Learning the Bible is the most important thing you can learn.
    2. The Bible is completely true.
    3. Putting into practice what you learn from the Bible will keep you from many problems later in life.
    4. Our family loves the Bible!
- Take time to regularly evaluate your children's spiritual development. Think about the spiritual goals you have for your children and determine what actions need to take place today in order to accomplish those goals.
- Keep aware of what your children are being taught in their church classes. Ask your children's teachers for insight as to your children's spiritual growth. Be actively involved in reinforcing the importance of what they are learning from their teacher or club leader.

**Foundation
Rock 2:
The
responsibility
for children's
ministry
first belongs
to parents.**

Parents, you *can* take your rightful place. God will enable you!

Resources

Freudenburg, Ben F., and Rick Lawrence. *The Family-Friendly Church*. Loveland, CO: Group Publishing, 1998.
An excellent book that discusses the need for churches to transform from a church-centered, home-supported ministry to a home-centered, church-supported ministry. Special emphasis is put on how best to connect the home and church.

Hansel, Tim. *What Kids Need Most in a Dad*. Grand Rapids, MI: Revell, 2002.
Read this book for practical and inspirational advice and information about the challenging role of fatherhood.

Trent, John; Rich Osborne; and Kurt Bruner. *Parents' Guide to the Spiritual Growth of Children*. Carol Stream, IL: Heritage Builders, 2000.
This resource provides a treasure chest of ideas for parents.

Wallace, Eric E., and John H. White. *Uniting Church and Home*. Lorton, VA: Solutions for Integrating Church and Home, 1999.
Recognizing the discontinuity in terms of faith and formation and focus, Wallace and White seek to find contact between the church and home, and help facilitate renewal and rebuilding between them.

Notes

1. "We discovered that in a typical week, fewer than 10 percent of parents who regularly attend church with their kids read the Bible together, pray together (other than at mealtimes) or participate in an act of service as a family unit. Even fewer families—1 out of every 20—have any type of worship experience together with their

kids." George Barna, *Transforming Children into Spiritual Champions* (Ventura, CA: Regal Books, 2003), p. 78.

2. Grace Baptist Church in Santa Clarita, California, requires dads to work in the nursery. Dr. Mike Broyles, the church's minister of education, informs me, "We require that all parents of nursery-age children serve in our nursery one hour every month with their children. This sets a foundation that parents (and fathers foremost) are the primary teachers of their children."

CHAPTER 3

The Battle for Balance

The Content of Children's Ministry

Command your children to be careful to observe—all the words of this law.
For it is not a futile thing for you, because it is your life.

DEUTERONOMY 32:46-47

Deb, coworker: "Only five minutes for the Bible story?"

She was attending the VBS training at her state denomination association and wasn't sure she heard the trainer right. But then the trainer said, "If you are getting pressed for time, leave out the Bible story, because it's the application that counts." *Deb protested!*

Jerry, children's pastor: The children's conference speaker was introduced as one who was "going to share principles from the Bible." Yet, he only referred once in his entire address to a Scripture passage. *Jerry was unimpressed.*

Tomas, Awana club director: Our club was having a contest. Points were being awarded for several things, including bringing a Bible. When the director was encouraging them to bring one, a red-haired boy raised his hand. "Why do you want us to bring a Bible? We never use it." *Tomas was ashamed.*

Shaylinn, Sunday School teacher of 2s and 3s: "I always use a picture Bible to supplement the Sunday School materials. The children just don't have exposure to the Bible story to really learn it." *Shaylinn has extra work.*

Biblical truth. Application. Relevance. Some people are passionate about the first, while others love the second. To still others, relevance is the key thing. Which is most important? Which brings maximum impact?

Do you understand the difference?

- *Biblical truth is the foundation*—what Scripture says.
- *Application is the link*—how it may be used today.
- *Relevance is the measure*—how closely the biblical truth applies to a person's life.

Unfortunately, it is possible to have truth and application without relevance, or application and relevance without truth. To have a rock-solid children's ministry modeled on biblical principles, we must have *balance* between all three.

Ministry Approaches

Model 1: *Truth Without Regard to Relevance*

I remember the Sunday School materials I used when I was a kid: a 10- to 12-verse Scripture passage and a brief explanation of the passage—

that was it. The application just wasn't there, and my teacher didn't know to add it. On the other hand, I *loved* the take-home paper, because it had a two-row cartoon that I always read during the church service. All Scripture. No creativity. No application. Is that the best approach?

Figure 5

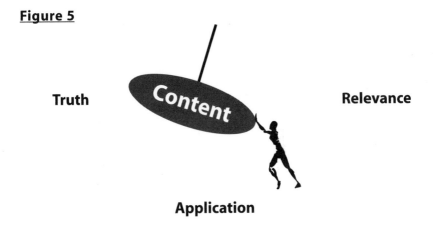

Model 2: Relevance Without Regard to Truth

The church puppet team had at least 30 different puppets. Puppeteers moved the mouths of the puppets with professional precision. The jokes were hilarious. The message? Be kind to others. No Scripture. No foundation of truth. Any Islamic imam, Buddhist priest, Jewish rabbi or anyone even slightly religious would have loved it. Even an atheist would have applauded.

Figure 6

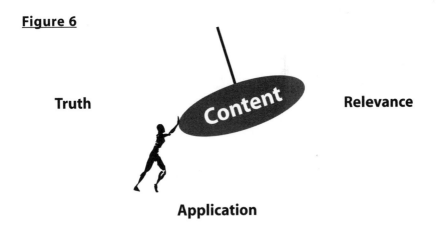

Model 3: *Truth* and *Relevance*

There is a great concern today, and rightly so, that teaching the Bible without making it relevant is only hollow, empty orthodoxy. Our churches have become champions of relevance and experts at it. But life application without a solid foundation of Scripture is equally danger-ous. Children's ministry without the bedrock of Bible truth is merely morality training. Let's keep it centered!

Figure 7

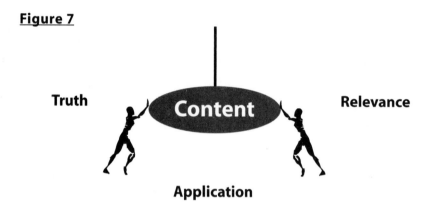

Balance is the best. And it comes through healthy tension. As we have voices crying for relevance in our materials, we must also have voic-es crying for an emphasis on the truth. When we balance both relevance and truth, children's spiritual growth is effectively nurtured. But where do we start? And how do we maintain the balance?

The Foundation Comes First

In 1982, my wife and I bought our first house. It was a real fixer-upper! We hauled 25 pickup loads of trash out of the house and yard. And then we painted, cleaned and carpeted. We made it relevant to our lives.

But we didn't touch the foundation. Think what people would have thought if we would have said, "We're remodeling our foundation." You just don't mess with that.

Children's ministry has definitely needed a new look, and changing the presentation is like painting the house—it's good. But we don't change the foundation. It's too important, and it's our first priority.

A respected Christian educator once summed up this principle with these words: "Truth without life leads to dead orthodoxy. Life without truth leads to heresy. Teaching one without the other is not biblical and is not the stimulus for spiritual growth."[1]

The Rock-Solid Model

Figure 8

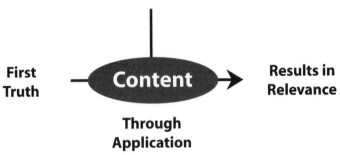

How do we mold a children's ministry that is centered and balanced? More than three thousand years ago, Moses gave us the principle: Scripture must be the main focus, and then relevant application will follow.

The Context

> Moses finished speaking all these words to all Israel, and he said to them: "Set your hearts on all the words which I testify among you today, which you shall command your children to be careful to observe—all the words of this law. For it is not a futile thing for you, because it is your life" (Deuteronomy 32:45-47).

The book of Deuteronomy is a second giving of the Law. In fact, the name "Deuteronomy" literally means "second law." The first Law (recorded in Exodus and Leviticus) was given at Mount Sinai. After the 40 years of wandering, Moses reviewed for the children of Israel the commandments of God (Deuteronomy 4—30). They were right at the border of

Canaan, ready to cross the Jordan, waiting for God's instructions.

Notice the context of this passage—what is before and what comes after.

BEFORE

In Deuteronomy 31:14, God said, "the days approach when you must die." Moses knew the time of his death was near. Then God dictated a song to Moses (Deuteronomy 31:19) to teach to the Israelites, and we can read the song in chapter 32. Once Moses finished the song (verse 43), he had some final words—his *last* words.

AFTER

> Then the LORD spoke to Moses that very same day, saying: "Go up this mountain of the Abarim, Mount Nebo . . . and die on the mountain" (Deuteronomy 32:48-50).

With these words, God told Moses that it was time for him to die. Earlier, God had told Moses he would see the Promised Land but would not enter it. Chapter 34, in fact, records Moses' death. Chapter 33 is not additional instruction; it is simply statements of blessing on the different tribes of the nation of Israel. Therefore, verses 46 and 47 are the final instructions of Moses.

These two verses follow this pattern:

Figure 9

Two Commands (46)	The Content (46)	Two Value Statements (47)
Set your hearts	all the words which I testify among you today	it is not a futile thing for you
command your children to be careful to observe	all the words of this law	it is your life

The Two Commands Concerning Relevance

Verse 46 contains the final directions that Moses gave to the children of Israel:

> Set your hearts on all the words which I testify among you today, which you shall command your children to be careful to observe—all the words of this law.

In Deuteronomy 4, Moses had begun his instructions with the same two commands:

> Only be careful, and watch yourselves closely so that you do not forget the things your eyes have seen or let them slip from your heart as long as you live. Teach them to your children and to their children after them (4:9, *NIV*).

From the beginning of the book of Deuteronomy to the end, Moses wanted the Israelites to be conscious of their prime responsibility to practice God's Word, and also to teach it to future generations so that they would obey.

The first command is "Set your hearts on all the words which I testify among you today." In other words, determine to live according to the words given to you. Obey them! But make sure it is not mere obedience. Set your hearts to obey.

Moses knew that parents' obedience came first.

The second follows: "You shall command your children to be careful to observe—all the words of this law." In other words, teach your children to obey from the heart as well!

Relevance at Its Best

What is relevant to you? How would you determine when something has relevance?

A. When kids think it's cool language
B. When it uses the latest technology or methods
C. When it applies to present-day issues
D. When it is fun for the children
E. When it produces obedience from the heart

Of course, it's *E*. I'm not arguing against the first four—in fact, they may be the means for accomplishing the last. But they are only the means and must not cloud the end.

Moses was concerned that the teaching of faith and obedience be ongoing. When that goal is accomplished, relevance is at its best!

Each of the commands has an object. Set your hearts—on what? Teach your children—what? The object is the content.

The Content—Truth

The content on which we should set our hearts and which we should teach our children is "the words of this law." Do you see? That's the foundation for application. The Word of God has to come first. Why do we start there? Because the words themselves are *truth*. Because they are *from God*.

I had the privilege of preaching in my church recently. Here's how the words of my sermon compared to God's Word:

The law of the LORD is perfect (Psalm 19:7).
    My words aren't perfect. God's are.

Your word I have hidden in my heart, that I might not sin against You (Psalm 119:11).
    My words aren't powerful enough to keep people from sin. God's are.

Forever, O LORD, Your word is settled in heaven (Psalm 119:89).
    The congregation has probably already forgotten my words. God's are eternal.

Through Your precepts I get understanding (Psalm 119:104).

Only a few of my words are wise. God's are all wise.

My word . . . shall not return to Me void (Isaiah 55:11).

I try to speak purposeful words. God's are always purposeful.

Your word is truth (John 17:17).

I find out later a sermon illustration is wrong. The words of God are always true.

All Scripture is given by inspiration of God (2 Timothy 3:16).

My words are a lot of interpretation, illustration and opinion. God's are authoritative.

The word of God is living and powerful (Hebrews 4:12).

It is the words of God that are alive. Can't say that about mine.

So why am I always so captivated with what I (or others) say, and not so enamored with the Word of God?

If you are a teacher (and if you're a parent, you are one), your application of spiritual truths is important—even essential. But without the Word as the foundation, your applications are mere morality training.

Start with Scripture. We must not only teach children *about* the Bible and how to *apply* the Bible, but we must also as first priority teach them *the Bible*.

What Does This Mean?

- *The priority of God's Word affects every teaching opportunity.* Not that you begin your lesson plan with Scripture every time, but it is your foundation. God's Word is where you start when you study.
- *The priority of God's Word affects every ministry.* How effectively will our students learn Scripture from the content presented in our

programs? How is the balance between truth and application of the truth? Probably you're thinking your ministry is pretty well balanced. But are you sure? Is that just your perception, or have you evaluated it carefully?

· *The priority of God's Word affects teaching at every age.* We must do more than give Scripture a cursory glance. We must major on Bible truths from early childhood through ages 9-11. As truths get firmly established in a child's belief system (the foundation of the house), then the relevance (the framework of the house) is solid.

We must *always* provide a foundation of truth, no matter the age of the child.

We must *always* make truth relevant, no matter the age of the child.

Build the foundation early. Make it solid. Then add the framework so that your students can "live in the house you built."

The Value Statements

Two value statements follow in Deuteronomy 32:47. These statements refer to the "words of this law"—God's Word.

For it is not a futile thing for you, because it is your life.

The first value statement is "It is not a futile thing for you." In other words, you won't be wasting your time! Parents and children's workers rarely see progress in a child's faith and obedience as fast as they would like and are tempted to wonder, *Is the result worth my hard work?* These words from Deuteronomy 32:47 are crystal-clear encouragement that persistence in the spiritual training of children *is* worth it. Our efforts are *not* pointless!

Who needs this reminder? The nursery worker, who regularly sings Scripture songs to the babies. The sixth-grade boys' Sunday School teacher, who wonders if the boys are really understanding. The parents of the 13-year-old who is beginning to challenge his family's beliefs and standards. And the Awana worker, who has never been told thank-you once in 10 years of helping kids memorize Scripture. Instilling God's Word in the hearts of children is a years-long process—we must not be discouraged!

The second value statement further intensifies the importance of following Moses' commands. About the process of verse 46, he adds a startling value statement, "*it is your life.*"[2]

Proverbs 4:20-22 (*NIV*) repeats this thought:

My son, pay attention to what I say; listen closely to my words.
Do not let them out of your sight, keep them within your heart;
for they are life to those who find them and health to a man's
whole body.

What does it mean to say that the words of God are your life? There are three possible implications.

First, it can imply a main focus. If you were to say about your son, "Baseball is his life," what would you mean? You would mean it is his main focus—what he thinks about all the time. For him, it is priority number one. Baseball has the highest value to him.

Second, "it is your life" can mean that something occupies all of your time. You might complain, "My work is my life," meaning that your work fills too much of your schedule.

Third, "it is your life" can indicate a matter of life and death. My father-in-law suffers from an advanced stage of sugar diabetes. He has to give himself an insulin shot four times a day. He doesn't miss a shot, because, for him, the insulin shots are a matter of life or death. He has to take them. We could say about my father-in-law's insulin shots, "They are his life."

This is also true of the air that we breathe. It is our life. If we don't have it, we die. So is water. Food is also our life. These things are absolutely necessary to our existence.

This is the best meaning of Moses' declaration that the Word of God is your life! It is a matter of life and death—spiritually speaking! That gives God's Word the highest value of all, and it only follows that the action of teaching God's Word to the next generation receives an equal rating!

Of course, when Moses said these words, he was speaking to the nation of Israel. Unfortunately for the Israelites, their descendants forgot his words just a few generations later. During the time of the judges, a generation grew up that did not follow God, and the nation died spiritually. The church of Jesus Christ today is only one generation away from extinction as well. If we were to stop teaching the next generation the Word of God, Christianity would die. It *is* a matter of life and death! It is a matter of life and death to our faith, to our churches, to our families and to our nation.

"It is your life." It is impossible to more highly express a value! There is not a way to ascribe to something a higher value than to say about it, "it is your life." And the context is clear: This value is placed only on the Word of God!

The Word is what is valued—not the packaging, not mere application—*the Word*. It must come first. It must be the foundation—the center, the core—of children's ministry.

Do you see how central the Word of God is?

Take what to heart?	The words of God.
Teach your children to obey what?	The words of God.
What is not idle words?	The words of God.
What "is your life"?	The words of God.

The Implications

We are in a battle for balance. If you haven't figured it out by now, this chapter is an appeal to make scriptural teaching the core content of children's ministry and *then* to balance it with life application and relevance.

Teaching then is guiding and declaring, guiding pupils and declaring truth. A real teacher does not hesitate to declare truth in a context of guidance. But if he only declares, he becomes a preacher. A teacher must be skilled in guiding, directing, helping pupils in their learning.[3]

What to Do

In chapter 2 of this book, we saw that parents have the primary responsibility to be the spiritual teachers of their children. This passage expresses your goal: that your child will obey God's Word from his or her heart.

"But my child doesn't have time to memorize Scripture—there's too much homework." Or, "We just can't seem to find time to read the Bible." Those are expressions of *value*, not *time*. But they are not the values that God desires.

Think about it: What should have a higher value than learning to obey God's Word? Which is more important:

Athletic skills or ministry skills?
Exercising the body or exercising spiritual muscles?
Memorizing multiplication tables or memorizing verses?
Good grades or godly character?

Parents, take seriously your responsibility to teach God's Word to your children.

1. Model obedience to God's Word yourself. It's just too important to leave to others. Your own attitude toward God's Word cannot be hidden from your children. They will know how you act, and that will be far more influential than what you say.
2. Put teaching God's Word first! It is never an issue of *time*. It is always an issue of *value*—and Scripture tells us that teaching our children God's Word must receive the highest value of all. If you put teaching God's Word first, you will find that there will be time left for other things. Will you change? Will you treat the spiritual training of your children as if it is a life-or-death matter?

Children's ministry leaders, guard the core content of your ministries.

1. Examine your curriculum. Does relevance build on a foundation of Scripture, or is the scriptural foundation absent or

minimized? Is it all Scripture, with no connection to life?

2. Watch the effort of your workers to keep up with current trends or the newest idea or the latest technology. Do the teaching methods crowd out Scripture, or enhance it?

3. Observe your teachers' practices. What comes first in their minds? Is it evident that the Bible is presented to children as foundational, authoritative and inspired?

4. Evaluate the scriptural understanding of your children. Find out what they are really learning. Can they name all the characters in the latest Christian children's video (no slam intended), but not the major Bible characters?

5. Review the allotment of time: How much is spent in actual hands-on Bible use by children versus other activities in your various ministries? Does it reveal the proper balance?

Children's workers, demonstrate the high value of God's Word.

1. Always use a Bible when teaching. Hold it in your hands often (insert your teaching guide in your Bible). Especially when teaching young children, let them see you teaching from the Bible.

2. Think about what excites you in your preparation. Is it the puppet? The game? The illustration? The activity? Or is it God's truth? In your preparation, take time to think about the significance of the lesson's Scripture in your own life so that what you are teaching is rooted in your own study and experience.

3. Demonstrate an attitude of awe and respect when talking about the Bible or its content. Emphasize that the Bible is true. Wait for children's attention before reading from the Bible.

4. Evaluate what impresses the children. It will be natural for them to enjoy the puppets, or the game, or the video, the most. What can you do to impress children with your presentation of Scripture?

5. Look for evidence of life change that comes from the heart. That's your objective! During classroom activities, how do children demonstrate their love for God and others?

Can't you just imagine Moses—knowing he is going to die—thinking, *What can I say to these people that will really make a difference?* His very last words to the children of Israel reveal the answer.

We have a huge job. Research tells us that the number of Christian young people with a biblical worldview is rapidly declining.[4] Yet we have *never* had more Bibles or more Christian materials than we have today. The problem is not one of resources—or opportunity.

We are in a battle for balance. Scriptural truth—or relevance? We *must* have both, but truth must come first! We have to start there.

Moses, by the inspiration of God, concluded this: the Word of God is so important that *it is your life*.

Is it yours?

Foundation Rock 3: Scripture is the foundation of our content; relevance follows.

Resources

Blankenbaker, Frances. *What the Bible Is All About for Young Explorers*. Ventura, CA: Gospel Light, 1986.
This book is a unique resource for both children and adults that shows how everything from Genesis to Revelation fits together. The book helps teach Bible study skills that kids need to grow in Christ.

McDowell, Josh. *Children Demand a Verdict*. Carol Stream, IL: Tyndale House, 2003.
Use this book as a reference to help you answer over 70 significant questions kids ask about God and faith.

Notes

1. Lois E. LeBar, *Education That Is Christian* (Wheaton, IL: Victor Books, 1989), p. 106.
2. Some translations say, "they are" rather than "it is." In both renderings, the reference is to the words of God that Moses had communicated. However, this statement must also include the associated actions of verse 46 of obedience and teaching future generations.
3. LeBar, *Education That Is Christian*, p. 173.
4. "Only 3 percent of the nation's 13-year-olds have a biblical worldview, which serves as the foundation for their decision making." George Barna, *Transforming Children into Spiritual Champions*, (Ventura, CA: Regal Books, 2003), p. 37.

CHAPTER 4

It's a Matter of Time

The Pattern for Children's Ministry

And these words which I command you today shall be in your heart. You shall teach them diligently to your children, and shall talk of them when you sit in your house, when you walk by the way, when you lie down, and when you rise up. You shall bind them as a sign on your hand, and they shall be as frontlets between your eyes. You shall write them on the doorposts of your house and on your gates.

DEUTERONOMY 6:6-9

5:30 A.M.	Alarm rings. Joe gets up.
5:45 A.M.	Joe wakes up Melanie. Melanie gets up.
6:00 A.M.	Joe gulps breakfast; then leaves for work by 6:10. Melanie gets dressed.
6:45 A.M.	Melanie wakes Nathan (first grade) and Jennifer (third grade) and then gets them dressed.
7:10 A.M.	Melanie wakes Joshua (the baby); then feeds the kids fast. Melanie prays with Nathan and Jennifer between bites.
7:30 A.M.	Melanie takes Nathan and Jennifer to the bus stop. Joe has his first meeting at work and deals with upset boss. Joe gets call from Sunday School director—agrees to teach next Sunday.
7:45 A.M.	Melanie plans Joshua's first birthday party.
8:30 A.M.	Melanie takes Josh to babysitter; then goes to part-time job.
1:00 P.M.	Joe has 10 minutes for lunch.
1:45 P.M.	Melanie finishes work, eats in the car and gets car lubed before picking up Josh.
3:10 P.M.	Nathan and Jennifer come home and eat a quick snack.
3:45 P.M.	Melanie gathers up the three kids and takes Jennifer to soccer practice and Nathan to piano lessons.
4:30 P.M.	Piano lessons are done. Melanie goes back to soccer field. Melanie takes kids to Burger King.
5:15 P.M.	Joe gets home. The house is empty. Joe makes a sandwich and mows lawn.
5:30 P.M.	Melanie gets home. Jennifer showers. Nathan whines. Joshua smells. Joe is still mowing.
6:30 P.M.	Melanie has worship team practice at church. Joe watches the kids, who watch TV.
7:45 P.M.	Joe finds out Jennifer has homework when he tells them to get to bed.
8:45 P.M.	Melanie gets home. Nathan is in bed. Jennifer is finishing homework. Joshua is asleep on the floor. Joe is asleep on the sofa.
9:30 P.M.	Melanie finishes her grocery list, wakes up Joe and then goes to bed.
10:30 P.M.	Joe catches up on sports scores; then joins Melanie.

When Joe climbed into bed, he shook Melanie's shoulder. His words were so telling: "How was your day, honey?" "Busy" was all she could answer. It was their first time to talk, to con-nect—when she was almost asleep.

Joe and Melanie are fictional (but typical) Christian parents. They want their kids to grow up to follow God. They enjoy a decent income and have a pretty good marriage. They are regulars at church. Yet, if sta-tistics prove correct, Nathan, Jennifer, or Joshua—one of them at least, maybe two—will abandon their faith by age 25.[1]

What are busy parents to do? What could Joe and Melanie do differ-ently? Are they powerless? Are the results left to chance? Aren't a pretty good marriage, church attendance and a loving home enough?

Is your home like theirs? If *you* were asked to pick one word to describe your home life, would you pick "hectic," "frenetic" or "crazy?"

How are we to raise godly children? Is there a pattern in Scripture to guide us? What *is* to go on in a child's home—no matter the century, or the culture, or the economic situation?

God, through Moses, tells us.

The Context

You've already learned that Deuteronomy is the second giving of the Law. Moses reviewed it right before the children of Israel entered the Promised Land.

In Deuteronomy 5, Moses restated the Ten Commandments. But the core verses in Deuteronomy are 6:4-5:

> Hear, O Israel: The LORD our God, the LORD is one! You shall love the LORD your God with all your heart, with all your soul, and with all your strength.

In fact, Jews call this the Shema—the central statement of the Jewish faith. It is as familiar to Jews as John 3:16 is to Christians. It immediate-ly precedes the commands to instruct children.

Notice what it communicates:

1. There is a God.
2. There is only One.
3. Our God is that One.
4. He deserves our best devotion.

These are four pretty important messages for Joe and Melanie to pass on to their three kids!

The Big Picture

Look at verses 4 through 9 as a unit. If you need to, read them again. Try to imagine the big picture that is being presented. There are two sections.

The *object* of family life (verses 4-5)—Families (both parents and children) who love the LORD with all their heart, soul and strength.

This verse is first addressed to parents, because their actions set the pattern of action to be followed. They have to model devotion to God themselves. In fact, the best way a child can learn to follow God is to have a parent who sets the example. Verse 7 makes it clear that these words are then to be passed from parent to child to grandchild; therefore, they also become the objective for the next generation.

The object of family life has little to do with the family's mind-set or skill sets (or the TV set) but rather with their "heart-set." The goal is not knowledge, material things or success. The goal is a deep conviction and a priority above all else: the development of the child's heart, soul and strength—in other words, the child's whole being. And in the child's development, his or her heart, soul and strength are to be directed toward God.

The Choice

Joe and Melanie knew that they must start with the time choices they make every day. They determined that their lifestyle would reflect their desire to raise children who were devoted to God. Of course, they realized that it must start with their own example.

The *environment* of family life (verses 6-9)—A lifestyle that impresses God's Word on children.

When you look at Joe and Melanie's schedule, do you get the picture of a home saturated with the teaching of God's Word? Taken together, these verses shout that the teaching of God's Word takes place all the time and everywhere.

What would a family be like that made the teaching of God's Word a priority? Here are some things that might come to mind:

- focused parents
- spiritual objectives
- directed schedules
- prioritized time

To Joe and Melanie, Deuteronomy 6:7-9 may have just sounded like *too much*. How could they possibly follow the pattern? At first glance, it seemed like this passage just wouldn't work today. If you are a parent, you may have had the same reaction as you read this chapter. But consider the benefits. There are many, but here are two important ones.

1. You greatly diminish the possibility of your children's involvement in sinful, destructive behavior in the future.

The psalmist said, "Your word I have hidden in my heart, that I might not sin against You" (Psalm 119:11). No parent *wants* their child to become an alcoholic, commit a crime, become addicted to pornography or abuse a spouse. And the psalmist's declaration not only was inspired by God, but it is also demonstrated in real life today. When God's Word is in the heart of a child (in other words, the child has a biblical worldview), it keeps the child from sin. If you could do something to keep your child from sin, wouldn't it be worth it? God lays out the pattern in Deuteronomy 6.

2. You greatly increase the possibility of your grandchildren's salvation and eternal destiny in heaven.

Here's the question: What kind of a family life will *you* need to have so that your *children* will have the kind of family life that results in your *grandchildren* trusting in God?

The psalmist Asaph encouraged us to teach God's Word to our children so that "the generation to come might know them, even the children yet to be born, and they in turn would tell their children. Then they would put their trust in God and would not forget his deeds but would keep his commands" (Psalm 78:6-7, *NIV*).

My father passed away nearly 30 years ago. My mother exemplifies the hope of eternity. Since both of them had trusted Christ as Savior, she plans to see my father again some day.

Usually, we only think about seeing our loved ones in heaven at the time of their death or when our death approaches. But we ought to think about seeing loved ones in heaven when we can do something about it! What you do today *can* make a difference in the lives of your grandchildren! Count on it: A God-centered, Scripture-based home will result in eternal rewards!

A Closer Look

How do you make this priority work every day? That is the big struggle for most Christian parents. They *want* to fulfill their responsibility of spiritually training their children, but life gets in the way: doctors' appointments, car repairs, in-laws visits.

The only difference for a family in Moses' day was the list: oxen sick, neighbors needed help, water jug broke. Just *life*. It gets in the way.

When and *how* can you find time to train your kids in the things of God is exactly what God reveals in these verses. You will learn:

1. Training must be formal and informal.
2. Training must be a lifestyle.
3. Training must include constant exposure to God's Word.
4. Training must include Scripture memory.

All the Time, Everywhere

Five-year-olds would have been the same in Moses' day. They just don't sit very still. And whether it's 3,400 years ago or today, sitting together at home with children takes deliberate action. It rarely just happens.

Think about the phrase "when you sit in your house" and consider the following:

- *It is planned.* Picture another family—Mom, Dad, 6-year-old Zebulun and 5-year-old Rebecca sitting at their home in Hebron in Moses' day, around the oil lamp, talking about God's Word. Taking the time for spiritual training wasn't easy then. And face it—spiritual training isn't going to get done today either unless you plan it.
- *It is structured.* You're not going to plan to sit at home and discuss God's Word for long before you ask, "What are we going to talk about if we do this regularly?" Planning leads to the need for an orderly approach.
- *It involves transmitting content.* Dad and Mom share from God's Word, Zeb and Rebecca listen. Dad says, "This is what God says." They learn the words of God.
- *It includes mealtime.* Guiding conversation around the truths of God's Word, especially with young children, is a way to use mealtime wisely! Focus especially on questions that guide basic worldview perceptions. Here are four questions that you can use regularly:

    1. What happened today that reminded you of God?
    2. What did you see today that reminds you that all people are sinners and need Jesus Christ?
    3. What did you hear or see today that did not agree with the truth in the Bible?
    4. What part of God's creation did you enjoy the most?

If Moses were writing the phrase "when you walk by the way" today, he'd say, "When you're in the car." This is the complement to what is communicated when you are in your house.

Think about the "walking" phrase and consider the following:

- *It is unplanned.* Zeb and Dad walk their sheep. "Look at that stone, there, Zeb," Dad points. "Doesn't that crack look like a letter? Remember the Ten Commandments were written on a stone. Can you remember one of them?"
- *It is unstructured.* Whatever the moment offers, there is always training that can be done. A stone, the actions of someone nearby, the weather—all become teachable moments, opportunities to link Bible truth to everyday life.
- *It involves applying content.* Dad and Mom make the Word of God live. "Did you see that man try to cheat? We don't do that because God's Word has told us to be honest. Zeb, do you remember what it says?"
- *It includes any time.* Here's how we did it recently when we had dinner with our three young grandchildren:

"Hey, kids, I had something neat happen today. I went to get the oil changed in the car, and it cost $17.71 (we had a coupon). I gave the man a twenty. Now how much should I get back?" Tyler, the oldest, said, "About three dollars." "Well," I said, "he wasn't thinking. He gave *me* $17.71—a whole lot more than I was supposed to get back. Wasn't that cool?" We waited. Travis, age 7, and Tyler, age 8, began to protest. "You should have given it back." "Why? What does God say?" pursued their mom. "That's like stealing, and God says, we must not steal." They got it. And, then I assured them that I did give the money back and got the right change.

An Appeal for Balance

We've just got to have both!

Figure 10

**Planned/
Structured**

**Spontaneous/
Unstructured**

Planned, structured teaching times are not enough! The teaching will become an academic exercise with little application to real life. Neither can parents only be spontaneous—without a planned approach, they are likely to miss communicating important truths.

Children's ministry and, consequently, children's materials can easily become too focused on relevance and application.

Yet teaching children the words of God "in your house" without making them relevant "by the way" produces hollow orthodoxy. We produce children who win Bible quizzes and always have the answer in Sunday School but never bother with how Scripture should guide them on Tuesday at soccer practice.

But relevance "by the way" without the words of God "in the house" is equally dangerous. Moral teaching without a firm foundation in absolute truth is mere relativism—no different from any other worldview.

Figure 11

Truth

Relevance

How Your Church Can Help

While this passage is directed specifically at the home, it has implications for children's ministry and the church as a whole.

- Encourage parents to have a systematic approach to training their children. Pick a Bible reading or devotional plan, and encourage your families to use it. Build a churchwide accountability and encouragement system for parents.
- Make sure the parents see the take-home materials provided with your curriculum. Set up an incentive for the child and parent to talk about the lesson: "If you bring back this paper with your parent's signature to show that you've read this paper together, you will get . . . "
- Develop a Training in the Home support network. Discuss with the leaders of your adult Bible studies and small groups how together you can plan small groups and Bible studies to encourage the learning of God's Word in the homes of the people in your church.
- Conduct children's ministries that model ways for parents to teach children about their faith. Provide opportunities for parents to observe skilled teachers who can demonstrate conversation that helps children connect Bible truth with everyday situations.
- Use a curriculum that provides a solid long-term plan for teaching the Bible to children. Moving from one curriculum to another, writing your own curriculum for a year, etc., make it less likely that all key Bible stories and foundational theological concepts will be covered.

A Consistent, Continuous Lifestyle

When You Lie Down, and When You Rise Up

Travis and Tyler, my two young grandsons who share a bedroom, love to talk after they get in bed and before they fall asleep. That's probably what Moses was talking about here. Remember, houses weren't nearly so big in Moses' day. Some were simply tents. People didn't have separate bedrooms. Usually there were only two or three rooms, so it would have been easy for the whole family to talk together as they were falling asleep.

What's the point? Review and reflection at the end of the day. Moses mentions that first. Then he mentions the beginning of the next day—when you get up. Why? For preparation for the new day.

Do you understand the pattern? Teaching God's Word is to be the dominant lifestyle characteristic in the home. It is to fill what we do.

Constant Exposure to the Words of God
Bind Them as a Sign on Your Hand, and They Shall Be as Frontlets Between Your Eyes.
What does "them" refer to in this verse? What is being addressed is the commandments—the words—of God. According to Jewish tradition, sometime possibly after the return of the Jews from exile in Babylon and Persia, the Jews began the practice of binding small leather boxes—frontlets, which are called phylacteries or *tefillim* today—with straps on their hands and on their foreheads. In the boxes, they would place small pieces of paper with this passage and others written on them. Jesus referred to this practice in Matthew 23:5. Devout Jews to this day continue their literalistic interpretation of this passage.

Have you ever worn a WWJD (What Would Jesus Do?) bracelet? The purpose of the bracelet is that you'll see it and be reminded by it. You see more of your hands than any other part of your body. *Others see your forehead.* Keep Scripture before your eyes in what you do, and keep it visible to others through what you do.

Signs play several roles in our lives. They give us important information. In each new country I travel, I'm very interested in knowing what the sign is for the men's restroom! It's very important information to know! The information on other signs isn't so welcome, such as Detour Ahead, but it is still important information. Treat God's Word like important information.

Signs also carry some inherent authority—No Trespassing or Keep Off the Grass! will instill immediate guilt in a violator, even though no penalty is indicated. Once *Candid Camera* put outside a grocery store a mat that read "Wipe Your Feet." Most people obeyed just because they felt a duty to follow the sign! Treat God's Word like it is authoritative.

Write Them on the Doorposts of Your House and on Your Gates

I love the plaque that quotes Joshua 24:15: "As for me and my house, we will serve the LORD."

The doorposts and the gates are the last thing you look at when leaving your home and the first thing you see when entering. This establishes an identity for your home and lets both your family and your friends know your family values.

Plaques in prominent locations in your home provide over months and years a continuous reminder of the purpose and foundation of your family.

How Your Church Can Help

Invest in quality plaques, posters or signs that relate to children's ministry and give these to parents. (Make sure the content is Scripture, not just nice sayings.) Take-home projects the children make will most likely stay on the refrigerator for only a few weeks. Give more long-lasting gifts to parents (e.g., CDs, audiocassettes and DVDs of Bible stories and songs that can be played or viewed).

Scripture Memory

I became committed to Scripture memory in seminary, when I found great edification in memorizing 1 and 2 Timothy and Titus. As a longtime staff member for Awana, memorizing Scripture has continued to be a regular habit for me and my family. But my memorization of God's Word didn't start when I was in seminary. When I was a young child, my mother insisted I memorize the verse that appeared each month on a Christian ministry calendar we received. Today I still remember most of those verses.

One can't study Deuteronomy 6:6-9 carefully without being impressed with the duty to communicate the very words of God to children and to ingrain those words and concepts into their hearts. The essential discipline of Scripture memory enables us do this. With memorizing God's Word, we can:

- talk about God's Word and what it means and ways to obey it when we "walk by the way;"
- keep Scripture constantly before our eyes (mentally);
- meditate on God's Word before we fall asleep and when we wake up.

"Don't forget to . . . " These are three of the most prominent words in any parent's vocabulary. That's simply what memorization is—helping your child not to forget something important: God's Word. But memorization is not just instant recitation. When Dad tells Junior, "Don't forget to take out the trash" and Junior replies, "I'll take out the trash," the process isn't finished. It is only finished when Junior actually takes out the trash. Memorizing God's Word is like that. We must recite, but then we must review so that there is long-term retention and obedience. Many Christians have memorized John 3:16 and can recite it accurately upon request—that's long-term retention.

How Children's Workers Can Help

- Evaluate the Scripture memory requirement in the curriculum you use. How are verse discussion, memory and review included? If these elements are not included, add them.
- Give parents a list of passages to be memorized. Encourage them to spend time with their children, both in learning the verses together, talking about what the verses mean in everyday life and in reviewing the verses.
- Show the value of God's Word by memorizing Scripture yourself and letting the children you lead and teach know specific situations in which Scripture memory helped you.

How Parents Can Evaluate

Parents, here's a test. How do you measure up to Deuteronomy 6? Mark each statement True (T) or False (F).

My children see learning God's Word as a lifestyle. __

We regularly balance formal instruction with informal application. __

God's Word is kept constantly in view in our home. __

My children are retaining key verses of Scripture in their memory. __

We model obedience to God's Word. __

Foundation Rock 4: Spiritual training of children is the core lifestyle of the home.

Moses said, "Impress them on your children" (Deuteronomy 6:7, *NIV*). Then he gave the pattern that would impress God's Word into the hearts and lives of children.

Parents, you can do it today. You can impress your children with God's Word! While God puts before you a huge challenge, He will also enable you to live as He wants you to live. Henrietta Mears, the founder of Gospel Light, said "not your *responsibility*, but your response to God's *ability* counts" (emphasis added). [2]

Just be diligent.

And God will use you.

Resources

Tripp, Tedd. *Shepherding a Child's Heart.* **Wapwallopen, PA: Shepherd Press, 1995.**
This classic book is balanced, in-depth and practical; the adjectives could go on and on. Get it!

Wright, Norman H., and Gary J. Oliver. *Raising Kids to Love Jesus: A Biblical Guide for Parents.* **Ventura, CA: Regal, 1999.**

Read this resource for great insight by two best-selling authors. The book is wonderful for anyone—teachers, leaders or parents—who works with kids.

Notes
1. H. Norman Wright and Gary J. Oliver, *Raising Kids to Love Jesus: A Biblical Guide for Parents* (Ventura, CA: Regal Books, 1999), pp. 11-12.
2. Henrietta Mears, quoted in Eleanor Doan, *431 Quotes* (Ventura, CA: Regal Books, 1970), p. 5.

CHAPTER 5

Avoiding the Millstone

The Warning About Ministering to Children

*But whoever causes one of these little ones who believe in Me to stumble,
it is better for him that a heavy millstone be hung around his neck, and that
he be drowned in the depth of the sea.*

MATTHEW 18:6, *NASB*

The Kids Who Never Came Back

He attended Sunday School once with his friend's family, but wasn't offered a ride again.

The children's leader kept forgetting her name, and then was overheard making fun of how it sounded.

The day he came, the Children's Church leader was having a Bible drill—seeing who could find the verse the fastest. He sat through the whole thing empty-handed. No one even offered him a Bible.

The children's worker's touch became too invasive. It left her feeling violated and fearful.

His dad always praised him for his baseball skills but never said a word of encouragement about his spiritual growth.

Her small-group leader had only two voice patterns—the monotone "Listen to me teach" and the high-decibel "Sit down and listen!"

They are the unaccounted for, the abandoned, the forgotten. While we are busy counting how many children we minister to, we neglect to count those who never come back. When they stumble, we rarely even notice.

How many children in America are exposed to the Church and to the gospel—even participating for a time, but then never come back? I don't know. But I do know that we are losing too many!

My travel to a missionary conference in Ghana, West Africa, required that I receive a yellow fever vaccination. A vaccine is a fascinating thing. It actually contains some of the dreaded disease microorganisms that are either weakened or dead. But rather than getting sick, our bodies react by producing antibodies, thereby creating immunity.

An infection with a disease is bad—but infection with God's Word is good. Immunity to a disease is good—but immunity to God's Word is bad. However, all around us are people that have been immunized to the gospel as children—because they got just a little bit that was either weak or dead—and there was no real "infection" at all. They never came back.

God has some strong words for those who do things that "immunize" children from coming to Him.

The Context

In Matthew 18, Jesus was responding to the disciples' question, "Who then is greatest in the kingdom of heaven?" (verse 1). They weren't thinking how pompous their question was, but Jesus was about to tell them.

To answer the question, Jesus used a little child as an object lesson. He had the child stand among them, and then said three things about children.

1. Children exemplify faith that saves: "Unless you are converted and become like children, you shall not enter the kingdom of heaven" (verse 3). A child *believes*. We'll discuss this more in chapter 8.
2. Children exemplify humility that pleases God: "Whoever then humbles himself as this child, he is the greatest in the kingdom of heaven" (verse 4).
3. Children test our authenticity: "Whoever receives one such child in My name receives Me" (verse 5).

A child helps us understand greatness. The disciples' faces were no doubt pretty red as Jesus responded to their question.

We might have the same tendencies as the disciples. We might be less thoughtful to the cleaning lady at work than we would be to our boss. We might ignore a homeless person but not someone we perceive as wealthy.

I remember a time I exhibited the same tendency as the disciples. I was playing golf. I hit my best drive of the day down the left side of the fairway. My playing partner lost his ball, so it was several minutes until we reached the place where mine should have been. It was not there, but two boys were just inside a backyard nearby. I asked them if they had picked up a ball, and they confessed they had. One went over and got my ball out of a bucket and sheepishly brought it to me. I embarrassed my partner by giving the boys a merciless lecture on golf etiquette. *I never would have said those things to an adult!* I saw the boys as more vulnerable, less apt to retaliate, and so I let them have it. I saw them as *least* rather than as *great*. It's not a memory that I'm proud of.

That is the context. Jesus used a child to illustrate that God sees greatness differently from the way we do. Having ended His object lesson with a child, Jesus then issued a warning.

The Action

But whoever causes one of these little ones who believe in Me to stumble.
MATTHEW 18:6, *NASB*

Of course, the stumbling that Jesus refers to is spiritual, not literal. It means to fall down spiritually in a way that results in sin—and lack of faith, particularly, according to the context.

- Jesus specifically mentions *believing* little ones—so the primary application is to causing those who have already trusted in Him to "fall down."
- But a secondary application is to those who have not yet believed. In that case, the "stumbling" may prevent them from coming to Him in faith.

Picture a child on the right path, making progress but never reaching the destination. The child stumbles and falls to the ground, because something trips him or her up and the child is unable to continue, or is unmotivated to continue. That is Jesus' picture.

My concern is, What might cause a child to stumble—to reject Jesus Christ or to fall down in his or her Christian walk? We'll discuss this question, but first let's focus on the warning.

The Warning

It is better for him that a heavy millstone be hung around his neck,
and that he be drowned in the depth of the sea.
MATTHEW 18:6, *NASB*

In other words, you're better off dead than to be someone that causes a child to stumble.

A millstone is a round circular stone, about two feet in diameter, used to grind grain. What is described in this verse was actually a form of capital punishment in Egypt, Rome and Greece during the days of Jesus. Jesus, though, adds to the imagery. He says "a heavy millstone"—indicating a stone different from the typical stone used for grinding grain. He was referring to one much bigger that would be turned by donkeys. If either size was tied around your neck and you were thrown into the ocean, you'd end up dead. His listeners had no doubt heard of the practice and, therefore, would be impressed by Jesus' referral to the "heavy millstone." It would be parallel to us saying today, "He swatted the fly with a sledgehammer." It was overkill (literally)—to drive the point home. Don't cause a child to stumble and to abandon his or her faith!

The contrast with Jesus' next warnings is interesting. In verse 8 He says, "If your hand or foot causes you to stumble, cut it off and throw it from you. It is better for you to enter life crippled or lame than having two hands or two feet, to be cast into the eternal fire."

Do you see it? If what *you* do causes *you* to stumble, you're better off maimed! But if what *you* do causes *a child* (anyone, really) to stumble, you're better off dead!

I'm ready to take this verse seriously. But how *do* we cause a child to stumble? To understand, we will look at examples of stumbling blocks from other passages of Scripture.

Stumbling Block 1—Neglecting Spiritual Training

The first stumbling block follows the verses that describe the pattern for the spiritual training of children (see Deuteronomy 6:6-9). Look for the stumbling block in these words from Deuteronomy 6:10-12:

> So it shall be, when the LORD your God brings you into the land of which He swore to your fathers, to Abraham, Isaac, and Jacob, to give you large and beautiful cities which you did not build, houses full of all good things, which you did not fill, hewn-out wells which you did not dig, vineyards and olive trees which you did not plant—when you have eaten and are full—then beware,

lest you forget the LORD who brought you out of the land of Egypt, from the house of bondage.

These verses describe Canaan, the Promised Land. The land was also called a "land flowing with milk and honey" (Exodus 3:8). When the Israelites conquered it, they were the sudden owners of land and crops—life was suddenly easy.

What's the stumbling block? The comfortable life—or the desire for it—can cause us to neglect our duty to teach God's Word to our children.

Throughout the world, where are Christian parents most committed to spiritually training their children? I don't know of any research data. But from what I've seen, parents in other countries, such as Cuba, Ukraine, India and Nepal, far surpass the typical Christian parent in North America in their commitment to spiritual training. We generally want our children to have things easy. And when things are easy, or at least comfortable, we lose the urgency to train our children in the things of God.

Stumbling Block 2—Undervaluing Children

Matthew 18:10 (*NASB*) says:

See that you do not despise one of these little ones.

Two Sixth Graders

Karen was our pastor's daughter. Kind, unselfish, smart—the list of her positive characteristics was nearly unending. We used her as an assistant leader in Awana; she helped in many areas of the church. Her commitment to Christ was (and still is) a wonderful testament to her parents.

Billy didn't know his father, his mother worked two jobs, and he and two siblings raised themselves. Billy came to our church and immediately made his presence known. He was loud, smelly, disruptive and obnoxious—he was every teacher's nightmare in the flesh.

I was the youth pastor. I loved to have Karen around. But I didn't feel that way about Billy. Now, I wanted him to come to church—to hear the gospel and respond—but to be honest, I didn't want that to take place at *our* church. Why couldn't he go somewhere else? He was just too much work.

Nearly every children's ministry has a Karen, and nearly every one has a Billy. Dealing with your Karen is easy, but your Billy will test your unconditional love and your commitment to faithfulness.

Isaac preferred Esau, Rebekah was partial to Jacob (see Genesis 25:28), and Jacob favored Joseph (see Genesis 37:3) and later Benjamin (see Genesis 42:4).

Jesus said, "See that you do not despise one." Not *most*. One. Every child is to be valued. We are to be entirely impartial. Why? Because every child is valued by our Savior.

Stumbling Block 3—Exasperating Children

Ephesians 6:4 (*NIV*) reads:

> Fathers, do not exasperate your children.

David's Failure as a Parent

The life of Absalom, David's third son, was a tangled, mixed-up mess, to say the least. This son of David provides some painful insight about what an exasperating father looks like.

Here is a short version of the story out of 2 Samuel (see 3:2-3; 13–18:33):

> Amnon, David's oldest son (Ahinoam was his mother) "fell in love" with Tamar, a half-sister (Maacah was her mother). Absalom, David's third son, was Tamar's full brother.
>
> Amnon's "love" was really lust—and he raped Tamar. His "love" turned to hate. When Absalom found out, he took Tamar in and cared for her. When David found out about the rape, he was furious.
>
> But David did nothing. Do you shudder at that like me? *His daughter was raped.* He did *nothing*—not as a father; not as a king.

And he *should* have—*he* was the judicial head of Israel! The law was clear: Amnon should have died for what he did to Tamar. Reading between the lines, I wonder if Absalom and Tamar thought, *Why doesn't Dad do something? Exasperation 1: Dad (David) abandoned his responsibility.*

The anger brewed in Absalom and finally boiled over—Absalom took justice for Tamar into his own hands and killed Amnon.

David then wouldn't forgive Absalom, and Absalom fled the country for three years. When he came back to Jerusalem, David wouldn't see him for two more years. *Exasperation 2: Dad refused to forgive.*

David finally agreed to see him, but for Absalom, it was too late. He had lost all respect for his father. He began to plot to overthrow David. The tragedy ends with Absalom being killed by David's men.

The most anguishing words in the Bible are perhaps David's words of mourning over the death of Absalom. I suspect David's grief was over not only Absalom's death but also the realization that he had failed as a father:

O my son Absalom—my son, my son Absalom—if only I had died in your place! O Absalom my son, my son! (2 Samuel 18:33).

Absalom's exasperation with David may have extended back into his childhood. Absalom grew up in Jerusalem in the palace. Two passages are also revealing about his childhood years:

Over and over again, 2 Samuel 8 describes the actions of David. Verse 13 is so telling: "David made himself a name." He was so busy with his career that there was likely little time for his sons and daughters. *Exasperation 3: Dad was too busy.*

Absalom would have been a young man when David committed adultery with Bathsheba and had Uriah, her husband, murdered. Neither action would have been possible had David not been king. David abused his God-given authority to satisfy his own lust. *Exasperation 4: Dad abused authority.*

When as a young man David was anointed as king, he was a man after God's own heart (see Acts 13:22), and he continued to enjoy that reputation. David, of course, wasn't perfect—but his heart was right. Absalom likely saw a different David—he saw his father's hypocrisy. While enjoying his fine reputation in the world, his father fell short at home. And unlike God, Absalom did not extend forgiveness and grace. *Exasperation 5: Dad was a hypocrite.*

Things haven't changed much for parents in three millennia, have they? We parents often struggle with the same issues David faced in his life.

1. Abandonment of responsibility
2. Failure to forgive
3. Too busy
4. Abuse of authority
5. Hypocrisy

Implications

For Parents

Restate this list in a way that identifies positive actions, and you will have a wonderful list of guidelines for dads and moms:

1. Take your responsibilities seriously and fulfill them.
2. Maintain harmony in the home through grace and forgiveness.
3. Make plenty of time for your relationship with your kids.
4. Find the balance between underusing and abusing your authority.
5. Be genuine and authentic in your walk with God.

For Children's Workers

This list is a great beginning for you as well. To keep from causing children to stumble, you must take the following actions:

1. Prepare well so that you can fulfill your ministry responsibility.
2. View children from God's perspective and extend grace and forgiveness.
3. Take time to build relationships with your students during class time and outside of class time.
4. Maintain a consistent and firm but positive system of discipline.
5. Live in consistent harmony with what you teach.

The Priority of Child Protection

The increased frequency of child sexual abuse incidents has elevated awareness of the issue in most churches and homes but, sadly, not in all. Sexual predators may find anonymity and trust in children's ministries in churches. The devastation sexual predators bring to a child and to his or her family is immeasurable. It is essential that all churches take action to remove this stumbling block from children's ministry.

Devastation Level 1

Central Church was the victim of a child predator. He was a Sunday School teacher who was trusted completely by church leaders and parents. At a Sunday School party, the predator established a relationship with a young boy that led to a series of clandestine meetings in which the abuse occurred.

Over the months and years after the abuse came to light, Central Church was nearly bankrupted by legal costs. There was no reserve fund. Many members and regulars tired of the additional financial burden and simply left for another church. The church annually struggled with finding insurance and was forced to go for periods of time without it.

The pastor and elders were exhausted. One elder counted 50 extra meetings in the first six months. The elders had no energy left for creativity or for new ministry—it was nearly more than they could do to simply keep their heads above water.

The church was dishonored in the community. Though the negative press died out in time, people still would respond to church members, "Oh, you go to Central Church? Isn't that the place where the child got molested?"

Church attendance plummeted. Morale suffered. Only after a name change and a location change years later did the church begin to recover.[1]

While every church that suffers with child abuse may not suffer this level of devastation, the potential always exists. A lack of diligence in screening, checking backgrounds and training is nearly a death wish for churches.

More concern is especially needed in smaller and rural churches, where people feel they know everyone—and therefore such diligence isn't thought to be needed. That is exactly the situation a predator is looking for!

Unfortunately, it often takes an occurrence of child abuse to awaken a church to action. But this devastation is not the most severe.

Devastation Level 2

The Gibsons' pastor called them to say he had something extremely serious to discuss with them.

He and the youth pastor met them in his office. Their world shattered as their pastor revealed that their 12-year-old son had confided with the youth pastor about his abuse by a trusted Sunday School teacher. The news could not have been more catastrophic for John and Mary Gibson.

John Gibson didn't sleep well for years afterward. Nightmares were regularly part of his early morning hours. Sometimes, the anger and fury would boil to the point of secretly wanting to kill the child predator. The justice system's punishment just didn't assuage the hurt that he felt. But he was most concerned for his son—and every time his son was out of his sight, the upset stomach and the worry would dominate each hour until they were together again. It took 10 years for John to accept the fact that his son was now safe.

Mary Gibson became a different person overnight. She cried daily, became jumpy and would snap back at her family for no apparent reason. Like John, she was drowning regularly with thoughts of regret, *If only I had been more alert* and worry, *Is it still happening with someone else that we don't know about?* Like John, she too wanted to control every minute of her son's life—in order to protect him.

The grandparents were also devastated. The other Gibson children became untrusting and cynical about the church.

The predator's family (in this case, a married man with children) was equally affected. His wife divorced him. His children disowned him. His mother, everyone said, went to an early grave because of it. Many innocent people suffered in various degrees the rest of their lives because of the selfish, sinful, uncontrolled lust of one person. [2]

Still, this is not the worst.

Devastation Level 3

Matthew Gibson innocently thought his Sunday School teacher wanted to be his special friend. But as their relationship got more and more intimate, he became more and more uncomfortable. The predator warned him not to tell—even told him that his little sister would be harmed "in a way you would never want to see her hurt." Matthew became two people—trying to hide his shame and his fear when he was with others, and scared to death when he was by himself. His youth pastor (also a friend of the family), upon watching him withdraw more and more, encouraged Matthew to tell him what was wrong. Matthew summoned all his courage and poured out his soul.

Matthew never returned to Sunday School. In fact, he avoided all Bible teachers from that time on. After a few months, he urged his parents to go to another church. They obliged, but when he was 16, he quit attending completely. He regularly attended counseling, but eight years later, some of the open wounds from the trauma remained unhealed. Matthew saw sex as something dirty and when he married years later, he struggled to have a normal relationship with his wife. He was overprotective of his children, refusing to ever allow a babysitter to care for them. It put a heavy load on his wife, which in turn strained their marriage.[3]

The hurt just continues. Like a pebble dropped in a pond, sexual abuse causes waves of pain that continue to move outward. It is no wonder Jesus said it's better to have a millstone around your neck and be thrown into the sea.

But this still isn't the worst. The critical issue is not just how many people are affected in this life but rather how many people are affected in the next.

Devastation Level 4

This incident affected the eternal destiny of many of the people involved. Church attendees, community members, the Gibson's youngest daughter and Matthew himself all rejected the Christian faith because of this incident.

We can identify with the physical and emotional pain that someone suffers, because we can *see* it and we can *feel* it. But Jesus' point is targeted toward the eternal. Physical and emotional loss can last for a lifetime—even for several generations—but our eternal destiny is settled *forever*.

Some churches are never motivated to protect children until their pocketbook is affected; for others, not until they are embarrassed.

Thankfully, others protect children because of their genuine concern for children and their understanding of the potential consequences if they fail in protecting children.

Why does your church have child protection policies and procedures? If it doesn't, why not? The devastation that is brought on a child, a family, a church and a community ought to be reason enough.

But the greatest reason is this: because the faith of a child may be hindered, preventing the child from coming to Christ! An eternity in hell is infinitely worse than child abuse here on earth!

Foundation Rock 5: Every child is safe and loved at all times.

Even thinking or reading about the stomach-wrenching issue of child sexual abuse stirs any children's worker's emotions deeply. Because we live in a sex-crazed society, it must receive our most diligent attention.

But we must be motivated not only by consequences in this life but also by eternal consequences. We must not cause a child to stumble in his faith in Christ!

Remember the scenarios at the beginning of the chapter? They portrayed partiality, embarrassment, rejection, thoughtlessness and other more benign ways to cause a child to stumble. We forget, however, that any one of them can have the same eternal impact as child sexual abuse.

Does your stomach wrench equally for them?

Resources

Cobble, James F., Jr., and Richard R. Hammar. *Reducing the Risk II: Making Your Church Safe from Child Sexual Abuse.* **Matthews, NC: Christian Ministry Resources, 1993.**
This kit includes six videos, a reference book and a training manual.

Gospel Light. *Children's Ministry Recruiting Guide.* **Ventura, CA: Gospel Light, 2003.**
This helpful book gives advice and guidelines on recruiting and screening children's ministry volunteers, creating a safety policy, etc. Includes reproducible forms.

Hammar, Richard R. *Risk Management Handbook for Churches and Schools.* **Matthews, NC: Christian Ministry Resources, 1993.**
This book is full of content to keep your church as safe and free from legal risk as is possible. It is a reference manual for dealing with different issues that involve children's ministry today.

Parker, Marv. *Safe Place: Guidelines for Creating an Abuse-Free Environment.* **Camp Hill, PA: Christian Publications, Inc., 2002.**
This resource is full of well-researched guidelines, training tips and plenty of downloadable forms for recruiting and training.

Notes

1. This story is a fictional account. Any resemblance to actual events or people, living or dead, is purely coincidental.
2. This story is a fictional account. Any resemblance to actual events or people, living or dead, is purely coincidental.
3. This story is a fictional account. Any resemblance to actual events or people, living or dead, is purely coincidental.

CHAPTER 6

Five Loaves and Two Fish

Children Serving in Ministry

There is a lad here who has five barley loaves and two small fish.

JOHN 6:9

If we would just let them, most Christian kids would just love to serve God.

The Feeding of the 5,000

Andrew shouted to the crowd, "Does anyone have food? Anybody? The Master wants your food. Does anyone have food?" A little boy tugged at his leg. "Not now, little boy. I'm trying to find food—Jesus wants it. Does *anyone* have food?"

The little boy kept tugging.

"Hey—quit pulling on my leg." Andrew was getting bothered. A little voice responded, "I've got food," and the boy held out a small leather bag.

"What's that?"

"My food. You said Jesus wanted some."

Andrew looked at the bag. He could tell that it didn't hold much. "Yeah, kid, but that's not enough. Hey, everyone—doesn't *somebody* have food? Jesus wants food." He noticed that the little boy's shoulders slumped in rejection.

Andrew looked at Peter, who held up his empty hands, and then at Philip, who shook his head. He could see several of the other disciples walking throughout the crowd, and none of them had food either. "Somebody must have a way to get food," he hollered again.

The tug returned. The eager face looked up at him, "Let Jesus have my food."

"Well, OK, but I don't think Jesus will think it is enough."

The boy's eyes brightened. He literally led Andrew to where Jesus was. As they approached, Philip and the other disciples were coming back as well, all empty-handed.

"We can't buy food for all these people," Phillip was saying. "We just don't have the money." The disciples all looked at one another as if to say, "What more can we do?"

The little boy tugged on Andrew again. "I have a boy here," Andrew said to pacify him. "He has five loaves and two fish." The tugging stopped. "But I don't know what good that will do among so many people."

All eyes turned to Jesus. He reached for the little leather bag and took it in His hands. He looked down at the boy and gave him a big smile. Then He said to the disciples, "Have the people sit down."

And you know the rest of the story.

I like to "imagine between the lines" of Scripture—to try to picture what went on behind the scenes. And in this one, I see

- a little boy eager to serve with whatever he had;
- an adult who felt the boy's contribution wasn't enough;
- Jesus' willingness to accept the boy's contribution; and
- Jesus' ability to do much with the little that the boy offered.

Can Children Serve?

Of course, they can! Proverbs 20:11 tells us "even a child is known by his deeds, whether what he does is pure and right." So why not have those deeds be acts of service for God?

Even though Timothy was a young man, Paul's encouragement in 1 Timothy certainly applies to children as well: "Let no one despise your youth, but be an example to the believers in word, in conduct, in love, in spirit, in faith, in purity" (4:12). I can imagine Andrew "despised" the little boy's youth as well as his lunch. But Jesus saw that he had something to offer, and He multiplied its impact.

The Bible contains a number of accounts of children serving God:

- Samuel served in the Temple from the time he was a young child (see 1 Samuel 2:18).
- The little servant girl in the story of Naaman wasn't afraid to tell Naaman's wife about God's power (see 2 Kings 5:2-4).
- Daniel was young—possibly in his early teens or even younger—when he determined to stand for the true God (see Daniel 1:8).
- Joseph (see Genesis 39:9), and then years later, David (see 1 Samuel 16:12-13), were quite possibly teenagers when they demonstrated their commitment to God through their lives.

- With the guidance of the high priest, Josiah the king of Judah served God faithfully, beginning at age eight (see 2 Kings 22:1-2).
- And of course, Jesus—He was actively discussing Scripture in the Temple at age 12 (see Luke 2:42-49).

Here is an example of how a young boy in today's world showed his commitment to God.

Kevin, a second grade student at a local public school, was thrilled when it was his turn to be Star Student.

He spent a lot of time preparing a poster, cutting out pictures and words from magazines that described him, and filling out his personality profile questionnaire with great detail.

Finally the big day arrived. He brought in his sports trophies and favorite books and toys. He stood up in front of the class as his teacher went over the poster with him. She carefully avoided the picture Kevin had placed in the center of the poster. He quickly pointed to it and said, "That's baby Jesus in the manger!" He then turned to the class and said, "That's the real meaning of Christmas!" The teacher brought his attention back to the poster and kept reading the words on it. She skipped another word so Kevin pointed to it and asked, "What's that word?" She didn't answer, so he asked again, "Is that the word 'missionary'?" Again, he turned to the class and asked if anyone knew what a missionary was. He was delighted when one of his classmates knew the answer.

When he started reading his personality profile questionnaire to the class, Kevin listed his favorite books, one of which is his bedtime devotions book. "It's kind of like a Bible," he told the class. Soon, all of the other children were whispering about the Bibles they owned or what their Bibles at home looked like. Kevin also told them about his favorite songs, "Lord, I Lift Your Name on High" and "Shout to the Lord." "Those are Jesus songs," he said.

In the span of 10 minutes, Kevin had shared his love for Jesus and witnessed to about 24 second graders and his teacher.

Kevin served God. Yes, children *can* serve—and not just someday—children can serve *now*. Let's think this through together.

Elements of a Ministry to Children

Figure 12

At a previous church, I served as the children's ministry coordinator. Our children's ministry leaders were concerned with the balance of what we were doing, so we used the ministry wheel above to plot the primary functions of our regular children's ministries.

Our church, average-sized, had three ongoing programs: Sunday School, Awana Clubs and Children's Church. We discussed what each contributed to our whole ministry and then plotted them on the wheel, which then looked like this:

Figure 13

It immediately became apparent that we were missing worship and serving. We began retooling. Sunday School and Awana stayed the same. But Children's Church was transformed to focus on worship. Then, we designed a Sunday evening program called KIT (Kids in Training) designed to get our children involved in serving. Once refocused, our children's ministries looked like this:

Figure 14

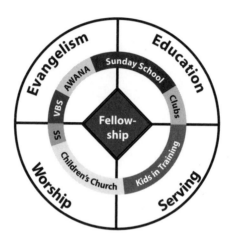

It was balanced. Our most glaring weakness, and our biggest challenge in fixing it, however, was building opportunities for children to serve.

Maybe you can identify with this situation. If your church needs to better equip children to serve, here are the reasons why it deserves your attention.

The Benefits

• Relevance—When children serve, they apply their faith.

I've never met a children's worker who didn't want children to apply their faith. Yet many struggle with making it actually happen. After all, if you only have them for an hour or two a week, how can you have that much influence? You can't create the opportunity for them to apply their faith—or can you?

Role-playing is a wonderful technique to include in your repertoire of teaching methods. But *real* playing is better. Get them involved in the real thing!

- Acceptance—When children serve, they feel part of the church.

    Quiz children on what they think the church is. Once you get past the perception of the building, you will find that they view the church as made up of adults. They aren't sure it truly includes them. The minimum age requirements for membership in many churches simply reinforce this. Children see the adults as the teachers and themselves as the "teachees." They aren't truly part of the church.

    The need to belong is very strong, especially for preteens. And nearly every church experiences a loss in attendance during those years. How can we be more effective in retaining our young people so that they feel like participants rather than spectators? If we want children to feel like useful, productive parts of the church, we must start involving them in service at a younger age.

- Influence—When children serve, other children are greatly affected.

    The Bible lesson was one of the worst I had ever observed—but at the same time it probably was one of the most effective I ever observed. The teachers did nothing to focus the attention of their students. There was no logical progression of thought, only random ones. The visuals weren't organized well. The teachers often stammered for the right words.

    But the children hung on every word. No one moved. You could see that they were visibly affected.

    Why then was the lesson so effective? The teachers were two fifth-grade girls, teaching their peers for the very first time. It wasn't the *message* that carried such force; it was the *messengers*. I seriously doubt that any of the other kids remembered what the teachers had said a month later, but I am positive that they remembered who said it.

    It's obvious: Children who serve greatly influence the children around them.

- Motivation—When children serve, they are spurred on to more learning.

    Have you ever engaged in a conversation with Jehovah's

Witnesses or Mormons who stopped by your door? Yes? Then I have one more question: Were you more motivated to study the Bible 10 minutes before you knew they were at your door or 10 minutes after they left? Exercise increases our hunger. And spiritual exercise will increase spiritual hunger in your children!

As children serve, they will begin to discover their own spiritual gifts. As they see God using them, they will be encouraged to continue to serve Him! You can't have better motivation than that!

• Permanence—When children serve, they are less likely to abandon their faith.

I still remember clearly my first experience in serving. Not too many opportunities existed for me, since I grew up in the sparse cattle country of north central Nebraska. There were no churches within 30 miles, so my family attended a small rural Sunday School, and I was the only child for several years. But at age 14, I was asked to help teach VBS in another community. I can remember two things: how big the responsibility seemed to me, and the children sidetracking me from the lesson and asking me questions about Christ's return. That was a pivotal point in my life; I began to internalize my faith. From then on, I had other opportunities to serve, and God cemented my faith in me. It became mine. My teenage years were far from perfect, but I never seriously questioned my faith or my relationship with God.

• Strength—When children serve with their families, the family unit is strengthened.

Like most problems, family strife almost always begins in selfishness. And service causes children (and their parents, too) to become others-focused rather than self-focused.

• Fruit—Children are often used of God to reach parents (and others) when alternate approaches are ineffective.

The children's choir at Christ Community, a church of 3,000, regularly sees adults come to Christ through their service. Before their ministry performance, which takes the whole worship service, the kids in the children's choir pray for family members who are unsaved to come, listen and respond to the gospel. Rarely does one of their services pass without several relatives of the children trusting in Christ!

The most effective thing we can do to keep our children and young adults is to get them involved in serving God at an early age.

Cautions

If we are to involve children in serving God, we must remember the following four points:

1. Service can't substitute for salvation.

 Serving God is of course for believers. That's why we held Kids in Training (KIT) on Sunday evening—a special time devoted to our core church families and their children. We felt we were more likely to avoid thrusting newcomers into roles that weren't for them.

 Children will volunteer, because they are eager to please. So don't ask, "Who would like to help with teaching the lesson next week?" Most will want to. Instead, ask, "If you would like to show God how much you love Him, come talk to me. I have an idea for you." Let the initiative be the children's, and let it come out of grateful hearts for what God has done for them.

 This answers the question, When should we get children involved in serving? The answer is, as soon as they are ready.

 "But I can't know the hearts of the children," you protest. You're right. But you can be careful what you say in talking about spiritual service.

When children are actively encouraged to serve God before they have trusted in Christ, a counterfeit Christianity is promoted—works without faith! Serving God and others always needs to be presented as a way to show love and commitment, never as a means of earning favor or salvation. This guideline is true for both the believer and the not-yet believer.

2. Service must begin with training.

One program idea that has impressed me is Kids Invite Training (another KIT). Ron Forseth of Outreach, Inc. has developed tools that train children to invite others.[1] I had never thought of that before! I had just *told* them to invite others, not *trained* them! His methods are proving highly effective and are a great reminder that children can greatly benefit from being trained to serve.

3. Service must involve the active participation of an adult mentor.

In fact, it must involve the important discipleship model:

   a. I will do it.
   b. I will do it; you watch.
   c. We will do it together.
   d. You do it; I will watch.
   e. You do it.
   f. You do it; someone else watches.

Because service begins with training, we must have adult mentors. Children need on-the-job training in which they are paired with an adult who understands the ministry. The role of mentoring adults—parents, or leaders and teachers at church—is essential.

Jehoash, who became king of Judah at age seven, needed the guidance of Jehoiada the priest: "Jehoash did what was right in the sight of the LORD all the days in which Jehoiada the priest instructed him" (2 Kings 12:2).

4. Service must not showcase natural talent.

You may have been around one—a child with unusual musical ability. The parents are Christians and desire that their child use his or her God-given ability to serve. But often, using such a child can do more harm than good because

- it may cause other children to think that you can only serve God if you are highly gifted; or
- it may stroke the child's ego more than it strokes his or her fire of passion for service. I've heard of three-year-old preachers (complete with three-piece suits), but I've never seen one. I've wondered, *What really motivates them?*

Ways Children Can Serve

The Home

Parents can intertwine their own service for God with the lives of their kids. The impact can be enormous! Here are some ideas:

- The Andersons occasionally took fruit baskets to their neighbors not only as an act of kindness but also as a method of building relationships that might lead to an opportunity to witness. Cara made sure that *her two daughters*, ages 6 and 8, *helped prepare the baskets* and then went along to deliver them. Her daughters got to experience the joyous and thankful responses of their neighbors and to hear their mother answer searching questions about Christ.
- The van Daahls's church had a campaign to distribute the Jesus video to every home in their small city. The *van Daahl children went along with their dad* to pick up the videos at the

church and then to hand them out in their housing development. They were timid at first, but by the third home, they wanted to run ahead and ring the doorbell themselves.

- The Ortiz family had one night a week when the *children took turns leading their family devotion time.* Even though the children were 5 and 8, they were eager to participate. Antonio, the 8-year-old, read the Bible story, and then asked the other family members questions, and Amanda, the 5-year-old, lead the prayer time.
- The Dahlmans collected clothing for a missions organization. They had their children, ages 9 and 11, *help sort the clothing.* Then, *they wrote little notes of love and encouragement,* which Justin, the 11-year-old, printed out on the computer. The notes were tucked into the clothing for the recipients to find.

The Church

What can children do to serve? Anything the adults do—with supervision and on their level. Here are some examples:

- At First Baptist, children 10 to 12 years old are trained to lead a Vacation Bible School program. Participation requirements are stringent and the training is vigorous. Then a team of children travels to another city, where the children, along with their adult sponsors, lead the games and the crafts, teach the lesson and share their testimonies.
- At Calvary Church, children are designated as hosts. When a new child comes, the host acts as the visitor's partner for the day, helping the visitor find his or her way around the facility and participating with the visitor in class activities.
- At Village Church, children do nearly everything in children's church—beginning with setting up chairs. Children run the sound system. Children take the offering. They lead in prayer. They read Scripture. They lead worship. All under the careful supervision and guidance of adults, of course—but they are learning to serve.

- At Christ Community, children are encouraged to complete the Kids' Evangelism Explosion course. As they complete it, they are encouraged to share Christ with their friends.
- At Grace Baptist, in place of adults reading Scripture, children recite the Bible passage for the morning as a part of the Sunday morning worship.
- At World Missionary Fellowship, families take turns leading worship. The children participate along with their parents, helping to choose songs and reading Scripture aloud.
- King of Kings Lutheran has a children's worship team that leads worship during the Sunday School time.

Foundation Rock 6: Children serve God as soon as they are ready.

Five loaves and two fish—to Andrew, it didn't seem like much. We can choose to view the contributions of our children in the same way, or we can see them as Jesus did— as enough to be used by Him in His way to accomplish His purpose.

Will you let them serve?

Resources

Gospel Light. *The Big Book of Service Projects.* **Ventura, CA: Gospel Light, 2001.**
Use this resource to find a wide range of service project ideas for use in the classroom, the church, the home and the community.

Note
1. For more information about Outreach, Inc., visit www.outreach.com.

CHAPTER 7

A Clear Focus

The Message for Children's Ministry

From infancy you have known the holy Scriptures, which are able to make you wise for salvation through faith in Christ Jesus.

2 TIMOTHY 3:15, *NIV*

"I'm a third year leader for the Sparkies [the Awana club for kindergarten to second graders], and it is such a joy to see them walk down the aisle at church to give their heart to the Lord. Or when they come up to me to ask if they can have Jesus in their heart. Don't give up on them. If you leave, you may miss one of your Sparkies walk down the aisle, because you gave up."

Emilie was 16 when she wrote that to me. She was obviously motivated in her ministry with young children and wanted to give them the gospel.

But what *is* the gospel? What saves a child? The Scriptures led Timothy to salvation, according to Paul—the Scriptures that he had been taught since he was an infant (see 2 Timothy 3:15). They are the source.

I've always been "camera-challenged" and as a result, I love the autofocus feature. It eliminates one way that I can mess up a photo—and believe me, I need that help. When I point my camera at what I want to capture on film, I push the autofocus button halfway down. Just like that, the camera reacts and brings the object of the photo into clear focus.

When it comes to sharing the plan of salvation, we must be on autofocus. As those who work with children, we must become so familiar with the gospel that we bring it into *clear focus* automatically, just as my camera does.

In this chapter, we are going to look at Bible passages that will guide us in understanding how to accurately share the gospel with a child. Children *can* understand the gospel when we make it clear—it is that simple! And we must present the gospel in its simplicity—but simple does not mean easy, or quick!

The Gospel Defined

Romans 1:16 (*NIV*) says:

> I am not ashamed of the gospel, because it is the power of God
> for the salvation of everyone who believes.

The power is in the gospel. No gospel, no power. It is that simple. But what *is* the gospel?

It is *good news*—that is what the word means.

It is *truth*, or more specifically, truths.

It is *from Scripture*. Paul told Timothy he knew "the holy Scriptures, which are able to make you wise for salvation" (2 Timothy 3:15, *NIV*).

Here's the definition worded differently: What good news, which is scriptural truth, has the power to provide salvation to everyone who believes?

The Plan of Salvation Defined

Consider the bigger picture of salvation by studying figure 15.

The Plan of Salvation Includes

Figure 15

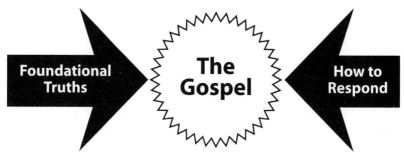

- All three must be communicated.
- All three must be communicated accurately.
- All three must be communicated repeatedly.

Foundational Truths

Foundational truths are essential for the gospel to take root. To a child who has no understanding of God's love, of his or her own sin or of

God's standard of holiness, the gospel is like the seed that fell on the path in Jesus' parable of the sower—it just laid on the surface and didn't take root (see Matthew 13).

What foundational truths need to be understood before the gospel can penetrate a child's heart? The Bible doesn't give a list. That is significant. Since God didn't give us a list, we can conclude that having an exact one isn't necessary. The Holy Spirit is the One who convicts of sin and a need of a Savior anyway. He may choose to bring a child to the Father at any point in the development of his or her understanding.

However, we aren't the Holy Spirit, so we must continue to instill in children the scriptural truths that He can use in the child's life. You may prefer a much longer list, but to provide a foundation for the gospel, teach children the following:

- Who God is (creator, holy, loving, just, etc.)
- What God demands (sinless perfection)
- Who we are (created, sinful, lost)
- What will happen to us (eternity in heaven or hell)
- Who Jesus is (God's Son, the sacrifice for sin)

Foundational truths come first. When a child understands these truths, fertile soil exists for the truths of the gospel to take root.

A child's upbringing will influence the time and effort needed to establish understanding of the foundational truths. Awana is partnering with New Tribes Mission in Papua New Guinea to create for animistic tribal children materials that teach Bible stories in chronological order. Why? Children in Papua New Guinea don't have the proper foundation. If you tell these children that Jesus is God, they will think He is a tree—or an animal. They won't comprehend the truth of the gospel. A proper understanding of the truth (God is the one true God who created all things) has to come first before the gospel can really be understood.

As contemporary culture confuses the Judeo-Christian foundation more and more, a similar approach may be more and more necessary to children in America. Does the child who visits your Children's Church for the first time really understand what we are talking about when we say "God"? The generation-old impact of *Star Wars* ("May the Force be with you") and other expressions that mold understanding of who God is has only intensified the challenge. If we move too quickly to a gospel presentation, will a child really understand?

The Gospel

The gospel must be the focus of our message to children. Foundational truths point toward the gospel. The child's response points back to the gospel.

We've already stated that the gospel means good news. But there is a lot of good news that won't save us: I'm a Chicago Cubs fan, and they won today. To me, that's good news, but it won't save anyone.

Neither are all the truths in the Bible part of the good news that saves. Jesus Christ is coming again—this is truth, but it is not *saving* truth. That truth may motivate you to salvation, but it won't regenerate you. Romans 1:16 says that there are truths that *save*. And together, they are the gospel.

The word "gospel" even refers to different things in Scripture:

1. The whole life and ministry of Jesus (see Mark 1:1). That's certainly good news. In fact, that's why the first four books of the New Testament are called Gospels. But do we need to know and believe all of it to be saved? No. Of course not.

2. The kingdom of God is near (see Luke 9:6 and compare it with Luke 9:2 and Matthew 4:17)! That was the message of the disciples when they were sent out by Jesus before His crucifixion, of course. That's not the gospel that brings us salvation, either.

3. The death, burial and resurrection of Jesus. This is the gospel! These verses clearly spell out the truths that bring salvation: "Now brothers, I want to remind you of the gospel

I preached to you, which you received and on which you take
your stand . . . that [Christ] died for our sins according to
the Scriptures, that he was buried, that he was raised on the
third day according to the Scriptures" (1 Corinthians 15:1,3-
4, *NIV*).

Dear reader, *that* is the gospel that has the power to save! It is these
truths that have regenerative potential! They are simple. Even a child can
understand them and act on them.

- Christ died for our sins (His work)
- He was buried (His humanity)
- He rose again (His deity)
- According to the Scriptures (His Word)

That *must* be the core message of children's ministry! The heart. The center. The nucleus. Everything else either points forward to the gospel or
is based back upon it. Saving faith is faith *in the truths of the gospel* and in
nothing else.

How a Child Must Respond

Think about it: If a child is to respond *to* the gospel, then it only follows
that the response is *not* the gospel.

In its essence, the response to the gospel is one of faith. In fact, if a
child's response to the gospel is *not* faith, then the child is not yet
saved!

Children's ministry is full of formulas for the plan of salvation. Each
of them is well intentioned. However, the Bible doesn't give us a formula. The Bible doesn't say there are four steps, or ABCs or any other recipe.
Formulas are often helpful to the new presenter, but they can be dangerous to a child: They can lead to an intellectual response (going
through the steps), not a heart response.

If we understand what the Bible says, then we won't need a formula.

Saving Faith Defined

Figure 16

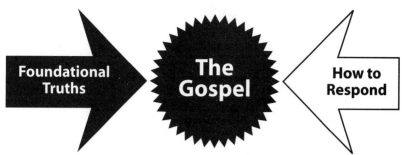

Children, and everyone else, are saved by God's grace through faith (see Ephesians 2:8). That's all. But what *is* saving faith?

Faith that saves must be in the person and work of Christ (see John 3:16; 3:36; Acts 16:31; Romans 10:10; 1 Corinthians 15:1-4). It cannot be faith in God in a general sense ("Believe in God") or in an action ("Remember, you wrote in your Bible when you became a Christian") or in good deeds. If the object of the faith is not right, it simply is not saving faith.

Some say, "Come to Christ." What does that mean to a child? Others say, "Give your heart to Jesus." Where is faith in that idea?

Telling children to believe in Jesus is not even clear enough. It's right but not complete. As presenters of the gospel message, we must focus children's faith on the person and the work of Christ on the cross. Faith must be in Jesus' death and resurrection.

"Wa-a-ait a minute," you say. "I asked Jesus to come into my heart when I was a child, and I'm saved." I believe you. It isn't right words that save us; it is faith. Your words, whatever they were, may have been an expression of faith. That's one issue. But another is what is said by the presenter of the gospel—and as presenters we have a responsibility to be as clear and biblically accurate as possible. We will confuse and mislead far fewer children if we are.

So what do you do? Repeat the gospel over and over again. Reinforce it regularly. Let your awe of it show through. Tell how and when you responded to it.

Saving Faith Described

We've defined the key elements of saving faith, but let's consider a deeper, richer description of what saving faith means.

1. It is *trust*. That's the best English word. Its meaning is more complete than "believe." "Trust" is the verb form of "faith." And the trust is active. As I write this, I am sitting on a chair. I believe it will hold me up. I have put all my weight on it. I trust it. That is what saving faith is—putting all your weight on Christ.

2. It is *trust* in the gospel—the death, burial and resurrection of Christ. Other objects of trust simply aren't adequate. Acts 4:12 (*NASB*) makes this abundantly clear: "And there is salvation in no one else; for there is no other name under heaven that has been given among men, by which we must be saved."

3. It is *trust* involving the whole person. With the *mind*, one *understands* the gospel. Yet by itself, this kind of faith will save no one. Children's workers and parents must be careful that they are not encouraging children to respond with their mind only. Some people call this "easy-believism," and it is a serious error. How do we know it's not enough? James 2:19 tells us that "even the demons believe—and tremble!" Demons would understand but not demonstrate saving faith.[1]

With the *heart*, one *agrees* with the gospel. I understand the arguments of other political parties, but I agree with mine. A Christmas present is under the tree—for me! I understand it is for me, and I agree with all my heart it is for me. I don't doubt it—I have faith. But the present isn't mine yet, is it? Understanding and agreement are essential but not sufficient.[2]

With the *will*, one *accepts* the gospel and *decides* to trust in Christ's death as payment for sin rather than trusting in something else. Help children understand the full meaning of the words "believe" and "trust."

What About Repentance?

The apostle Peter told the crowd, "Repent therefore and be converted" (Acts 3:19). Jesus spoke of repentance, as did Peter and Paul. Repentance is certainly biblical. Then, is repentance a second thing one must do to be saved? Is there one way but two steps? Is it trust *and* repent? No. If that were the case, John 3:16 or Ephesians 2:8-9 would include the word "repent." Rather, repentance defines saving faith further.

Repentance is not confessing a list of sins or merely feeling remorse over them. It is changing one's mind or direction—the literal meaning. In fact, we would understand Scripture more clearly if we would read "change your mind and direction" every time we read in the Scriptures the word "repent."[3]

Is this repentance? "I was going to arrive at 6:30 P.M., but I changed my mind and I'll get there at 7:00 instead." No, it's much more than that. It's like a person switching political parties or a vegetarian becoming a meat-eater. Suppose someone said, "I believe in Jesus as my Savior, but I'll keep depending on my own way to get my sins forgiven and to get to heaven." There is no repentance—no change of mind!

How Should We Describe Repentance?

Repentance (and therefore saving faith) is a decision—a change of mind—to no longer trust in yourself for salvation but to trust solely in Christ's death on the cross. Saving faith involves a decision—*repentance*. You see, there is *active trust*.

"Wa-a-ait a minute (didn't you say that before?), that sounds like something a seminary student would understand, but I'm not sure about my children. I'm not sure I know how to get a child to do all that." Remember, that's not your responsibility—it's the Holy Spirit's. But you must understand it. And you can be as clear as possible when explaining it.

Saving Faith Communicated

Clean Up Your Vocabulary

A kindergarten worker asked children if they wanted to let Jesus come into their hearts. Immediately, a five-year-old tilted her head back as far as she could and opened her mouth wide.

Another leader of six-year-olds related this prayer request from a child: "My uncle Tim is going to have his heart operated on. Can we pray that the doctor won't hurt Jesus?"

How we express the gospel can mislead children! Here are some phrases that you should eliminate from your presentation of the gospel— they are inaccurate, incomplete and/or for those who are already saved:

Figure 17

	Inaccurate	Incomplete	For the saved
Come to Jesus	✔		
Ask Jesus to come into your heart (or let Him in)[a]	✔		✔
Give your heart to the Lord[b]	✔		
Turn to Christ[c]		✔	
Accept Him as Your Savior		✔	
Pray to receive Christ[d]	✔		
Trust Jesus		✔	
Ask the Lord to forgive you of your sins[e]			✔
Confess your sins[f]			✔

[a] This phrase, found in Revelation 3:20, is addressed to the saved, the church at Laodicea, not the unsaved.
[b] Proverbs 23:26 is the only time a phrase like this is used, and it isn't in regard to salvation.
[c] "Turning" gives some idea of repentance, but where's the faith?
[d] It's not the prayer that saves anyone, it's the faith.
[e] He will when we trust in Him. But the Bible never expresses salvation that way.
[f] The only reference that tells us to confess our sins is 1 John 1:9, addressed to believers. Confession in Romans 10:10 is in regard to the deity and sovereignty of Christ, not our sins.

Don't Cut Out Calvary

When you talk about salvation, include the gospel message—Jesus' death and resurrection. Avoid these pitfalls:

• *Moving straight from sinner to faith*—"We are all sinners and are lost in our sin. Won't you accept Jesus now so that He will forgive your sin?" *No gospel.*

- *Moving straight from God's love to man's response*—"God loves you and wants you to come to Him today." Again, there is *no gospel.*

Don't Confuse the Child

Keep your message clear and simple. Watch out for these missteps:

- *Hiding the gospel with unclear invitation methods*—"Pray right now and let Him come into your heart." What really is a child to do? Pray? Pray what? Open their mouth? Or trust?
- *Hiding the gospel by connecting faith with specific actions*—As parents and teachers, we are *so* eager to *see* children respond! We forget that faith is something that takes place in the heart, not in the feet, the hands or the eyes. We say, "Raise your hand if you want to be saved." "Repeat this prayer . . . " Is it the *action* that saves? What might a child think if we associate an action too closely with faith? The feet or the hands can respond when faith is not involved!

Sharing the Gospel with Children

When sharing the gospel with children, *build the foundation,* and then reinforce it regularly. Rarely is there "single-contact evangelism." The Holy Spirit generally uses many messages and many instances to begin to draw a person (even a child) to Himself. We must be more concerned about the process of preparing children to receive and understand the gospel than we are about the point of response.

Repeat the message often. No matter what you are teaching, include the following eight truths regularly. Your students will learn well through the repetition:

1. God is holy (perfect and without sin).
2. We are sinners.
3. There is punishment for sin—death in hell and separation from God's love.
4. God loves us.
5. Jesus died on the cross and rose again.
6. His death paid the punishment for us.

7. If we trust in what Jesus did on the cross, our sins are forgiven.

8. God will give us eternal life.

Keep it simple, keep it accurate, and include it regularly. Let the Holy Spirit use your words.

Encourage them to trust in Christ. Tell children you will be glad to help them understand more, and if they would like to talk to you, you are available. Say this regularly.

Developing a Method of Invitation

Study the following chart of instances in Acts in which the gospel is given and then followed by someone's believing in Christ. Read the passage, and check out how the invitation was given. You'll see a very important pattern.

Figure 18

	People asked to respond with action?	People responded with belief?	Converts pressured to respond?	Converts demonstrated faith publicly?
Peter had just preached to a multitude in Jerusalem (see 2:37-47)	No	Yes	No	Yes
Peter preaches to the crowd in the Temple (see 3:12—4:4)	No	Yes	No	?
Philip witnesses to the Ethiopian eunuch (see 8:34-38)	No	Yes	No	Yes
Peter preaches to Cornelius's family (see 10:34-45)	No	Yes	No	Yes
Paul and Barnabas in Antioch (see 13:46-48)	No	Yes	No	Yes
Paul and Silas in prison in Philippi (see 16:30-34)	No	Yes	No	Yes

Not one time in these passages, or any other, did a teacher ask others to raise their hand, to come forward, or to perform any other physical action if they wanted to be saved. Neither was there pressure to respond. *Every time*, there is a reference to faith, or believing. There was a genuine, public response by the new believers—*initiated by them, not by the presenter.* And it is easy to see the Holy Spirit was the One at work convicting the people.

Practical Guidelines

I know you desire three things: (1) to see as many children as possible place their trust in Jesus Christ, (2) to avoid false professions as much as possible, and (3) to follow the biblical patterns.

Here's how to invite children to become Christians, whether they are your own if you are a parent or those in a group that you lead. But remember these four key guidelines:

1. Be biblically accurate in your choice of terms so that the children are not confused.
2. *Never* let a physical action (raising hands, standing up, praying a prayer, going to talk to a teacher or leader) be considered part of salvation by the child. Talking to an adult is certainly appropriate, but the child should understand that it is a way to learn more, rather than to become a Christian.
3. Let a child tell you what he or she wants to do—not the other way around. Ask that very question: "What do you want to do?" Don't just ask yes-or-no questions ("Do you know you are a sinner?" "Would you like to become a Christian?")
4. Watch for responses that might be motivated only by a desire to please you or another teacher, or be influenced by another child who is responding. In that case, ask, "Why do you want to talk to me?"

A Suggested Model

If you need to present a gospel invitation in a group setting, you can follow this pattern:

- Present the gospel message clearly and simply.
- Ask children to bow their heads and close their eyes while you pray. Thank God for His love and for sending Jesus to show God's love for us by dying on the cross for our sins. Briefly mention your gladness in knowing what Jesus has done to make it possible for each person to become a member of God's family. Thank God that Jesus is alive today.
- Have some announcements, or something brief, to change the atmosphere so that children do not respond from emotion.
- Ask the children who want to know about becoming a Christian to meet with the teacher or leader (you or someone else) when other children begin another activity.
- Ask children who responded why they wanted to talk to you or what questions they have about becoming a Christian. If children seem undecided about whether to talk or not, say, "I'm glad you're interested, but this is so important, I'm not going to decide anything for you. This is your decision." Answer questions by reading or quoting Bible verses. Use simple but biblically accurate terms, avoiding symbolic wording that is often misunderstood. State clearly that salvation comes from what Jesus Christ did, not from what they do. To help gauge children's understanding of the gospel, ask questions such as Why do you think it's important to become a Christian? What difference do you think it makes for a person to be forgiven? What do you think it means to become a Christian? What would you say to tell a friend about why God sent Jesus to Earth?
- Tell children that if they want to become Christians, they can pray to express their faith, but remind them that their salvation comes because of personal faith in Jesus Christ, not because of the words of a prayer.
- Ask children if they want to tell others about their decision—don't tell or force them to tell. When salvation is genuine, there is a desire to tell others—just like those new believers in Acts.

• Provide appropriate follow-up materials for parents and teachers.

While you read this chapter, did you wonder about your own salvation? Have you truly trusted in the death of Christ as the payment for your sins? Have you responded by faith with your mind, your heart and your will? Or were you relying on a physical action that took place at some time in the past?

Right now, salvation can be yours. You have learned what the Bible says—just respond right where you are. Jesus has promised, "whoever believes in [Jesus] should not perish but have everlasting life" (John 3:16).

As Christians, the gospel of Jesus Christ is our most precious intellectual property!

Proclaim it.

Protect it.

And keep the focus clear!

Foundation Rock 7: Children's workers communicate the gospel with clarity and urgency.

Resources

AWANA Clubs International, "Scriptural Evaluation of Salvation Invitations," 2004. http://www.bible.org/docs/splife/evang/ awana.htm (accessed October 4, 2004).
This document summarizes and evaluates a variety of questions that are often used in talking with children (and adults) about salvation. A helpful analysis based on Scripture is provided for each question.

Lutzer, Erwin W. *How You Can Be Sure That You Will Spend Eternity with God.* Chicago, IL: Moody Press, 1996.
This book doesn't specifically address the issue of sharing the gospel with a child, but it is very clear about what the gospel is.

Murphy, Art. *The Faith of a Child: A Step-By-Step Guide to Salvation for Your Child.* **Chicago, IL: Moody Press, 2000.**
Read this book for a thorough and Scripture-filled study of how to share the gospel with a child.

Notes

1. See also 2 Peter 2:21.
2. See Romans 10:10.
3. Try this technique with these passages: Matthew 3:2, Acts 3:19, Revelation 2:5.

CHAPTER 8

The Golden Hour

The Opportunity of Children's Ministry

Let the little children come to Me, and do not forbid them; for of such is the kingdom of God. Assuredly, I say to you, whoever does not receive the kingdom of God as a little child will by no means enter it.

MARK 10:14-16

The Golden Hour and the Silver Day

A serious car accident, a stabbing, gunshot wounds, severe burns, a long fall—victims of these accidents often are level 1 trauma patients. They need immediate, life-saving medical attention.

The best chance for survival for a level 1 traumatic injury occurs within one hour of the injury—the "golden hour." As a result, paramedics are trained to "scoop and run." Trauma center staff are prepared 24 hours a day. Monitoring and diagnostic equipment are always available, because every second counts. Emergency and trauma center personnel are so familiar with the term "golden hour" because they live out its urgent reality.

In the earliest citation of the term, Robert Locke says, "Time is always the enemy because patients in or near shock can die if not treated within "the golden hour" after the injury.[1]

Time is the enemy in the evangelism of the unsaved as well. But *is there a golden hour in evangelism?*

Some trauma surgeons have also proposed that in addition to the golden hour, there is also a "silver day"—a second but longer period of time that is also a window of opportunity critical to survival—the 24 hours after a severe injury.

The ages of 4 to 14 are the golden hour of evangelism. Research, anecdotal evidence and even common sense all clearly identify the childhood years as a window of opportunity for the greatest life-saving impact for eternity. For a large majority of people, if they do not respond to the gospel as a child, they likely will not do so later in life.

All the ages of youth form the silver day. The teenage years as well provide a prime opportunity to evangelize. God still draws people to Himself in adulthood, but the proportionate instances of spiritual rebirth are dramatically reduced.

The most critical window: childhood—the worldview-forming years. Then, youth—the years of decision. It's just thinking strategically. Reaching people while they are young is simply the most timely and the most fruitful.

What does Jesus say about this window of opportunity? He agrees. If you let them, little children will come.

Remember the setting of Mark 10? Peter, James and the others had rebuked the parents for bringing the little children to Jesus for His blessing. Their actions prompted Jesus' angry reply, "Let the little children come to Me" (Mark 10:14).

Afterward, Jesus sealed the point by taking the children in His arms and blessing them. Then He spoke. And every word of Jesus is significant.

"*Let* the Little Children Come"—the Command to the Disciples

Permit. *Allow*. Let them come. It's pretty clear.

Jesus scolded the disciples because they hindered the children from coming to Him for a blessing. But in the very next verse, He connected that incident with the spiritual issue of salvation. He made a spiritual application from the real-life experience. We can do the same.

The disciples didn't realize that they were doing something wrong until Jesus pointed it out. Parents or children's workers (see the following examples) can also unknowingly hinder children from genuinely coming to Christ.

The Inoculator

You know what an inoculation is. We talked about it in chapter 5—you get a little of the disease in a weak or dead form so that your body develops antibodies that will protect you when the real disease attacks. A weakened or dead presentation of the gospel may inoculate children from coming to Christ when they hear the real gospel message.

I was visiting an Awana program and conducting an evaluation for the leaders. The speaker was a Christian firefighter. He did a masterful job of demonstrating his equipment, weaving in his testimony and spiritual truths along with the demonstration. But he never gave the children the gospel or asked them to respond. The director got up, and I guess intended to give a salvation invitation. He began by saying, "How many of you kids would like Jesus to be your friend?" Of course, they all raised their hands. "I am going to pray, and I want all of you to say it with me." And phrase by phrase, he led them through a salvation prayer. The prayer was actually pretty good, but after it he inoculated the children: "Now, if any of you said that prayer for the very first time, *you are now a Christian.*"

No one is saved by saying the right words—in a prayer or otherwise! Salvation comes by *faith*—Ephesians 2:8-9 makes that abundantly clear! I imagined that none of those children was expressing faith when they parroted his words. Yet he told them they were Christians! How many of those children were inoculated against future teaching on the gospel, because they were told they were Christians by praying that prayer?

An inoculator, in enthusiasm to see kids saved, makes it too easy, and is too eager to confirm a child's decision. Salvation isn't *our* work, it's God's (see Titus 3:5)!

How *do* we make sure that our efforts at evangelizing children are not weakened or lifeless, like a vaccine? You'll get some ideas later in the chapter.

The Headhunter

Years ago, a friend leading a children's evangelistic campaign reported that in one week, more than 5,000 children professed to know Christ as Savior. I was amazed. Then he admitted, "We don't know how many of them were genuine. But if just 20 were truly saved, it was worth it."

What do you think? *Was* it worth it? Here's what I think: Yes, but . . .

As I've become more experienced in children's ministry, I've also become more concerned about the 4,980 who were told they were now Christians and, maybe from that point on, thought they were Christians, but no regeneration ever took place. Too great a concern with numbers can lead to bad methods. And bad methods can lead to deception that can affect a child's eternal destiny.

At times I have had the privilege of interviewing missionary candidates. One candidate wife, Susan (not her real name), told the following story about her salvation experience as a child:

I grew up in a strong Christian family. We attended church regularly, and every summer, we kids would attend the Vacation Bible School at our church. I was scared of one of the teachers who was a very large, loud lady. My parents later told me she would brag to others in the church, "No child ever comes through my VBS class without receiving Christ as Savior."

The year came when it was my turn to be in her class. I was petrified because my older siblings told me about her and what to expect. I didn't want to go, but my parents made me anyway. The loud lady's witnessing technique was to spend some time with each child away from the rest of the class, explain the way of salvation, and ask them to respond. The day came when it was my turn. I went with her, but I wanted my "turn" over as quickly as possible. "Susan, do you know you're a sinner?" "Yes." "Do you want to accept Jesus as your Savior?" "Yes." I was as agreeable as possible in order to get out of there fast. After she had me repeat a prayer, she had me write in my Bible, "Today I became a Christian" and then sign my name.

I knew I hadn't really become a Christian, but for a number of years, when I would voice my doubts, my parents or people at my church would remind me, "Don't you remember—you wrote it in your Bible?"

I finally trusted in Christ when I was 16.

Susan was hindered for several years because one well-intentioned lady was so concerned about her perfect record that she didn't consider the possibility that the decisions she encouraged might not be genuine. When the children said the right words and prayed the right prayer, she was satisfied—she thought she had added another trophy to her collection.

A headhunter, in concern to see many children saved, resorts to techniques that result in multitudes of professions of faith but not necessarily in genuine ones.

The Manipulator

The camp evangelist worked the kids into a fever with his humorous stories. Unfortunately, I still remember a gross one that had the children nearly convulsing with laughter. There was certainly no problem with his holding their attention! When the atmosphere was at its height of emotion, he moved at lightning speed, it seemed to me, to ask them to accept Jesus as their Savior. Many responded. But I wondered, *Did they respond because of their concern over their sin and their lost condition (that wasn't mentioned), because of their faith in Jesus' work on the cross (that wasn't mentioned either), or because of their emotional connection with the speaker?*

It's easy for a persuasive speaker to manipulate children. But the bottom line is that the Holy Spirit does the convicting of the need of a Savior.

We can use methods that *let* children come to Christ. They must never be manipulated.

Imagine a path. It is hidden with underbrush. Rocks are everywhere. A landslide has cut away a section. Now think of this as representing the path a child may take in coming to salvation. Jesus is not instructing us to pull the child through all the obstacles and over the rocks. What's implied? *The children will come.* Just be concerned about clearing the underbrush, removing the rocks and filling the gap left by the landside. When the path is clear, they will come. The Holy Spirit will lead them. Just don't *you* hinder them.

The Discipler

Each person described above means well but may fail to allow children to genuinely come to Christ. So can the person who is so focused on growing the baby Christian. The discipler can be so focused on the growth of the baby Christian that he or she forgets the baby must be born first!

My friend Dr. Greg Carlson was involved in a meeting with youth ministry leaders. He is still reeling from the comment of the leader sitting next to him, who said, "We discourage children's evangelism."

Scores of times I've heard comments like "this year we are teaching our children character qualities." What a good thing! But first it takes regeneration for Christlike character to develop. Our enthusiasm over a spiritual growth topic can cause us to forget to include the gospel.

It's popular today to say, "We intentionally shepherd our children at our church." If your church says that, make sure it's well defined and keep it up! (If your church doesn't say it, it should start.) Nurturing is appropriate and necessary. It is comparable to the watering, fertilizing and weeding of a garden—critical to healthy vegetables! The importance of shepherding and nurturing cannot be diminished. *But we musn't let it crowd out evangelism of children.* We must accomplish them both.

You're a Sunday School teacher. The lesson is on speaking kindly to others. You have 15 students. Thirteen are regulars; two are visitors that you don't know. Do you find a way to weave in the gospel?

You're a VBS instructor. The week is almost up. The kids have been wild for the last two days. You are running out of time to make a point! Do you shorten or eliminate the part about the gospel and talk instead about improving their behavior, or do you make sure to include the gospel even though some of the kids aren't paying much attention?

You're a parent. You want to reinforce what your kids are learning at church, so you ask them often what the lesson was about. When can *you* make a point of explaining the gospel to them?

You're a children's ministry director. You look for curriculum that is balanced, creative, easy to use, doctrinally in agreement with your church, educationally sound—and the list could go on. Is a clear, regular presentation of the gospel on your list?

Children can learn Bible stories, Christian songs, character qualities and godly behavior but never hear the gospel!

"Let the *Little Children* Come"— the Age of the Subjects

What do you do with an avid five-year-old evangelist? My daughter, Andrea, was just that. Andrea had professed to trust in Christ at age four. She told Marissa, her four-year-old friend from down the street, that Marissa needed to accept Jesus as her Savior. Marissa prayed with Andrea, but a day later, she told Andrea that her mom (a strong Jewish mother) told Marissa that they didn't believe in Jesus, so Marissa couldn't talk about Him again.

Another day, Andrea and her three-year-old brother, Ryan, were play-ing in her room. Andrea came out excitedly and announced "Ryan's a Christian now!" At *three years of age*. She had told him he needed to trust in Jesus as his Savior, and he did just what his big sister told him to.

Of the three, who was saved?

Andrea is now in her late 20s, and the evidence is in: Her love for God and her desire to serve Him from that young age to the present demon-strates that her faith in Christ was genuine.

Marissa moved away a year later. We can't judge her salvation, but probably, she was only pleasing Andrea that day.

Ryan didn't trust in Christ that day either. We knew he had only fol-lowed his sister's urging. We prayed for his salvation and continued to instruct him about the gospel. It was a number of years later that Ryan truly placed his faith in Christ. Ryan's life demonstrates it, too.

What about childhood conversions? And what about presenting the gospel to children in children's ministries?

The words "little children" prompt two critical questions for chil-dren's workers and parents:

1. Can young children be saved?

   Should we even be presenting the gospel and inviting them to accept Jesus Christ when their understanding may be limited?

   Some say no. Through the centuries, many theologians have believed that young children can't be saved. Even some who believe in salvation by faith have taken that position.

   But look at what Jesus said: He said their utter dependence and simple trust is *a model* of the kind of faith that saves. If it's a model, how can someone conclude that a child can't have that kind of faith? If a child's faith is exemplary, it is impossible to conclude that it is not developed enough.

   Some say yes, but . . . It's possible; however, childhood conver-sions should be discouraged.

   One of my acquaintances (a children's pastor) is emphatic that in his children's ministry, the teachers will not give invita-tions until the children are 11 or 12 years old. He feels children may respond because they want to please the teacher or because their friends respond. He has a valid point.

But the very real problem of children's responding for the wrong reason has more than one solution; to refuse to invite them to trust in Christ is simply not the best one!

But Jesus says yes—let them come. In the context of this passage, He relates the issue not only to a blessing but also to receiving *the kingdom of God*—salvation.

2. When should we present the gospel?

When do you start presenting the gospel to children in your church? Should we share the message of salvation to preschoolers? How about young primaries? Elementary? Just how old should children be when we urge them to respond to the gospel message?

When should Christian parents start explaining the gospel to their own children? Should they as parents teach it from toddler age or wait until the child has better ability to understand?

This verse helps us with the answer. Just how old were these children that Jesus was referring to? They were *little*. The word used for "children," even in Greek, the original language of the New Testament, is not just "children," it is "little children." This could mean anything from babies to elementary age.

As discussed earlier, parents traditionally brought toddlers to a rabbi to be blessed. The young age of the children is further implied when we read that Jesus held them in His arms (see Mark 10:16)—an action that is more likely with little children. When children get to be five or six, parents and others become less interested in holding them in their arms—the children are too big.

What's the point? It is these young children about which Jesus says, "For the kingdom of God belongs to such as these. I tell you the truth, anyone who will not receive the kingdom of God like a little child will never enter it" (Mark 10:15, *NIV*).

The concept of teaching Scripture in order to lead to salvation from an early age is sealed by 2 Timothy 3:15. Paul says to his disciple, Timothy,

> From infancy you have known the holy Scriptures, which are able to make you wise for salvation through faith in Christ Jesus (*NIV*).

Paul *doesn't* say when Timothy became a believer. But he *does* say that from *infancy* Timothy knew the Scriptures. Start to teach them early—as early as possible. Then let the Holy Spirit do His work.

"Let the Children *Come*"—the Response of the Children

Children *will* come to Christ. I've never met a young child who was an agnostic or an atheist. They are open, moldable and receptive.

Some adults will just come. The man with leprosy (see Luke 5:12-15), Zacchaeus (see Luke 19:1-10), Nicodemus (see John 3:1-21) and the Ethiopian eunuch (see Acts 8:26-40). Most have to be brought, like Simon (see John 1:35-42), confronted, like the Samaritan woman (see John 4:4-26), or shocked, like Saul (see Acts 9:1-19). But too many will not come at all.

Children are different. They will come.

Survey your adults. How many of them were saved as children? *Then ask those who were saved as adults—do you wish you were saved as children?* The answers you get, of course, will be a unanimous yes. It's just common sense: The earlier one comes to Christ, the fewer years are wasted.

The childhood years are clearly a window of opportunity—the golden hour.

I recently drove through Iowa on I-80. Some of the corn fields had been decimated by flooding earlier in the season—the yield per acre wasn't going to be much. But a few miles farther, on higher ground, the corn looked mature, tall and full of grain. Now suppose a farmer had a field in both areas, suppose the farmer spent a large amount of money and hired many workers to harvest the flooded field but spent only a small amount of money and hired a few workers to harvest the healthy field. We'd say the farmer was crazy.

Yet this is what our churches are doing.

Figure 19

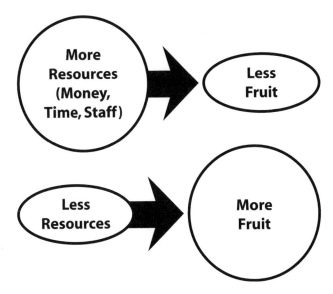

That is exactly what George Barna concluded from his research:

If you want to have a lasting influence upon the world you must invest in people's lives; *and if you want to maximize your investment, then you must invest in those people while they are young.* The research simply crystallizes lessons that we can observe through history and personal experience. In other words, if you connect with children today, effectively teaching them biblical principles and foundations from the start, then you will see the fruit of that effort blossom for decades to come (emphasis added).[2]

John Crupper, of Awana Clubs International, adds:

When seen from the perspective of eternity, this window of opportunity in which we have the greatest prospect of reaching individuals with the gospel must take on a compelling priority. . . . This is not to suggest that ministry to other age groups is not important or does not have its place within a larger ministry strategy. . . . In short, our expended efforts have not been commensurate with the available opportunity and the results that are possible.[3]

How do you see evangelism of children? How does your church see it?

- A subfunction of children's ministry?
- A seasonal event that takes place once a year (VBS)?
- A theme if a lesson plan calls for it?

Evangelizing children simply *is* the best use of our resources. It *is* the most fruitful. *More* of their lives are still before them. Follow-up and discipleship afterward *is* easier. It just makes sense. Evangelize children—because they will come.

Foundation Rock 8: Children have regular opportunities to trust in Christ.

Is your passion stirred? Can you see that time is our enemy? Do you sense the urgency?

We have no choice. We must light the fire in our churches and homes anew regarding evangelism of children. How about you? Your church? Is it prioritizing reaching kids with the gospel? No? Or not enough? Do you want to know where to start?

The major effort, energy and resources of a level 1 trauma hospital are focused on the golden hour and the silver day. If your church sees the urgency, and desires to focus as well, there are five standards you will want to set as goals.

Five Ways a Church Can Show They Believe Children Will Come to Jesus

1. The evangelism leaders will recognize the urgency of the golden hour and involve themselves in children's evangelism. The evangelism committee will guide children's workers in evangelism, not simply leave it to them.
2. The church budget dollars designated for evangelism reflects the comparative fruitfulness of children's evangelism. VBS and other evangelistic efforts to boys and girls will be a priority item when budget decisions are made.
3. Children's workers are fully trained in how to share the gospel with kids. Every children's worker is prepared and confident to share a biblically accurate, age-appropriate explanation of the gospel message.
4. Parents are trained to share the gospel with their children. They have the greatest opportunity to share Christ with their own child. Who better to be trained than the parents?
5. The church (especially the leaders) is as aware of and excited about a child's coming to Christ as they are about an adult's coming to Christ. Children who trust in Christ receive equal treatment and attention as adults who are new believers. Help the congregation share in the excitement of children's positive spiritual steps by briefly interviewing children after camp, after VBS and at the end of the school year. Interview children in the worship service or at other all-church events. Write articles for church newsletters that describe the ways in which children are benefiting spiritually from children's ministry programs.

The conclusion from nearly every perspective is that there is no better time to share Christ with people than when they are children.

Their lives are ahead of them.

Their worldview is being molded then.

They are open and receptive.

And Jesus said, "Let them come."

I will. Will you?

Notes

1. Robert Locke, "New Techniques Developed For Treatment of 'Epidemic'," *The Associated Press,* January 18, 1982.

2. George Barna, *Transforming Children into Spiritual Champions* (Ventura, CA: Regal Books, 2003), p. 42.

3. John Crupper, "Heralding the Priority of Ministry to Children Ages 4-14" (unpublished paper, Awana Clubs International, n.d.).

Building a Rock-Solid Model

Before you began reading this book, where were you in your attitude toward a Bible-modeled children's ministry?

- *Apathy*—I never thought about it. It wasn't important to me.
- *Acceptance*—I thought about it and liked the idea. But I thought I'd let someone else do it.
- *Affirmation*—I could really value it. I'm thankful that someone is doing something to get us back to God's Word as a foundation.
- *A priority*—This is worth my time, my energy, my effort. I'll *do* something!

This book is not intended for *recreational* reading. My desire is that it will prompt you to *action*—and *real change*, if change is needed. If God has moved you to pursue action through reading this book, you may need suggestions on how to proceed.

First, read it again—this time with a friend or coworker. As you read it, think about what action you might take!

Let's pick up the story of Joe and Melanie (see chapter 4). They're still fictional—but let's see how they would have made it happen in their church, if they were real.

Agree on the Need for a Model

Joe and Melanie met with the children's ministry coordinator, Judy. "We're parents, Judy," Joe began. "I've become convicted from God's Word that it's our responsibility to train our kids spiritually. But I need help! And I'd like it to come from the church." He told Judy about the Scripture passages that God had used to persuade him and Melanie.

Judy listened. *I wish every child in our ministry had concerned parents like Joe and Melanie,* she thought. God flooded her mind with questions about their children's ministry in general. *Are we supporting parents like we should? How could our workers be more effective in following through with the children? Was what they were doing aligned with Scriptural principles?* The conversation stirred in her a deep desire to think this through some more.

As they talked together, the conviction deepened in all of them that what they were doing with children needed to be based more firmly on biblical principles.

They agreed to set a date to meet with the senior pastor. Judy knew the benefit (and the necessity) of his support in anything they tried to do.

A week later, Judy, Joe and Melanie sat around a table in their pastor's office, and together they shared what each of them had come to realize—that they must be more Bible-based in how they were ministering to the children in their church. Pastor Scott encouraged them to put together a team of interested people, spend some time praying and studying, and then come back to him and the church leadership board with a plan for what they thought needed to be done.

Build a Team

Joe and Melanie began sharing their concern with other parents. They invited five couples to their home and asked them to study with them Scripture relating to the spiritual training of children. God began to help others, especially the dads, become aware of the opportunity they had to teach their children.

Judy used the next children's ministry leaders' meeting to present her concerns and to get their response. It was overwhelmingly positive: "Yes, we'd love to study what God's Word says about children's ministry. Yes, we *need* some standards to go by. Yes, we'd *love* just to be assisting the parents, not the other way around. Yes, our teachers *do* need training in sharing the gospel." Their comments confirmed to Judy that God was preparing the way for a new course of action. She challenged them all to look for resources and come up with ideas.

Make a Plan

As Joe and Melanie compared notes and prayed together with Judy, ideas just began to flow:

- Could we talk with some of our parents to find out just what exactly is going on?
- How do our elders view children's ministry? Could we involve them?
- Are our kids *really* learning the Bible? Is there a way we can find out what they know—a test or something?
- We don't want to offend our teachers. How can we get them on board?

They decided to focus on four areas in the following order:

1. Cast the vision—first, to church leadership; second, to children's ministry workers; and then, to parents.
2. Enlarge their network—find a "champion" for the cause in each children's ministry and in every adult small group that they could.
3. Begin with small steps—clearly define the issues; then address each one over a period of three months.
4. Set some measurements—so they could evaluate progress.

With the initial strategy in place, they went back to the pastor for approval.

Initiate Action

Judy asked Joe and Melanie to start a Parents' Support Group for their children's ministry. Peter, her children's club director, showed them a list of Rock-Solid Standards for Children's Ministry that he thought they could use.[1]

Pastor Scott agreed to study and prepare a series of sermons on raising godly children. He also agreed to encourage the elders to talk and plan with children's ministry leaders, and to enlist the elder's support for what Judy, Joe and Melanie were doing.

They decided upon promoting one tool—a children's story Bible that families could read together regularly.

Evaluate Progress

"How do we know this won't just fade away?" Peter asked in a meeting with Pastor Scott. "How can we make sure that this represents a permanent change in our church?"

"You need a system of accountability. It's got to be one kind for children's ministry and another for parents. For children's ministry, why don't you first set up a system of self-evaluation? Then, ask our sister church to send a group of its children's workers over to do a peer evaluation. That way, you will not only get a more objective perspective, but you might also encourage them to follow the same model.

"For parents, you'll need to either establish support or accountability groups, or else talk to our small-group directors about weaving it in to their current plans."

Three Sundays later, Joe and Melanie listened as their pastor preached passionately about the importance of children's ministry. They had seen the posters about teacher training on the way into the sanctuary. They watched as a number of parents signed up to participate in new support groups.

It's happening, Judy thought. *Thank God for Joe and Melanie! I think we're really on our way to getting our children's ministry based upon Scripture!*

Measure Your Progress

Below is a matrix for you to use.[2] Each of the eight principles is based on a chapter in this book. Each is listed, followed by four suggestions from the corresponding chapter as to how it might be accomplished in your church. A blank line is included for you to add your own suggestions. A rating scale is on the right.

Here's how to use it:

- Use the scale for a pretest with your children's workers. See how they rate your ministry right now.
- Self-test once every six months. Track your progress.
- Finally, use it as a tool for peer evaluation when you ask another church to come give you its perspective on how you are doing.

Determine to excel in each area. Feel free to add suggestions or to change what is there—but work to achieve the standard!

Figure 20

Rock-Solid Standards for Children's Ministry	Rating* 1 2 3 4 5

1. Ministering to children is a high priority.

- Children's ministry is included in church objectives. ○ ○ ○ ○ ○
- Children's ministry leadership enjoys a "peer status" with the leaders of other ministries. ○ ○ ○ ○ ○
- Church budgeting reflects a priority on children's ministry. ○ ○ ○ ○ ○
- Facility use and conditions reflect the importance of children's ministry. ○ ○ ○ ○ ○
- _____ ○ ○ ○ ○ ○

2. The responsibility for children's ministry first belongs to parents.

- Adults are regularly encouraged and equipped to relate what they are learning to their children at home. ○ ○ ○ ○ ○
- Children's workers deliberately act to involve parents in their child's spiritual education. ○ ○ ○ ○ ○
- Parents understand and take ownership of what their children are learning in the children's ministries. ○ ○ ○ ○ ○
- The majority of parents in the church place a high priority on the spiritual training of their own children. ○ ○ ○ ○ ○
- _____ ○ ○ ○ ○ ○

* 1—Always true; 2—True most of the time; 3—Sometimes true; 4—Rarely true; 5—Never true.

Rock-Solid Standards for Children's Ministry	Rating* 1 2 3 4 5

3. Scripture is the foundation of our content; relevance follows.

- Scriptural content is the primary criteria in choosing curricula. ○ ○ ○ ○ ○
- Children's workers consistently demonstrate the high value they place on God's Word. ○ ○ ○ ○ ○
- Learning biblical truth is the foundational objective for all ages. ○ ○ ○ ○ ○
- Relevance to life is the basis for application of Bible truth. ○ ○ ○ ○ ○
- _____ ○ ○ ○ ○ ○

4. Spiritual training of children is the core lifestyle of the home.

- A majority of parents regularly teach their children God's Word. ○ ○ ○ ○ ○
- Parents receive regular, specific training on how to integrate God's Word into their home. ○ ○ ○ ○ ○
- Materials for the home are promoted and made available to parents. ○ ○ ○ ○ ○
- Scripture memorization is a regular discipline encouraged in children's ministry and in the home. ○ ○ ○ ○ ○
- _____ ○ ○ ○ ○ ○

5. Every child is safe and loved at all times.

- The children's ministries have a consistent, positive and well-communicated system of discipline. ○ ○ ○ ○ ○

* 1—Always true; 2—True most of the time; 3—Sometimes true; 4—Rarely true; 5—Never true.

Rock-Solid Standards for Children's Ministry	Rating* 1 2 3 4 5
• Children's ministry workers are trained in how to build and maintain a healthy, proper relationship with their students.	○ ○ ○ ○ ○
• Child-protection policies and procedures are defined and implemented consistently.	○ ○ ○ ○ ○
• Parents are trained in how to discipline their children.	○ ○ ○ ○ ○
• _____	○ ○ ○ ○ ○

6. Children serve God as soon as they are ready.

• Opportunities abound for children to serve God in the church.	○ ○ ○ ○ ○
• Standards (including salvation) for those wanting to serve are made clear before children are offered the opportunity.	○ ○ ○ ○ ○
• Children receive training and close adult guidance for their ministry activities.	○ ○ ○ ○ ○
• Service opportunities help children to feel they are a vital part of the local church.	○ ○ ○ ○ ○
• _____	○ ○ ○ ○ ○

7. Children's workers communicate the gospel with clarity and urgency.

• Children's workers are trained in how to present the gospel.	○ ○ ○ ○ ○
• Children's workers can express the gospel message and how children are to respond with saving faith.	○ ○ ○ ○ ○

* 1—Always true; 2—True most of the time; 3—Sometimes true; 4—Rarely true; 5—Never true.

Rock-Solid Standards for Children's Ministry	Rating*				
	1	2	3	4	5
• Children are regularly presented with the gospel message and allowed to respond as the Holy Spirit prompts them.	○	○	○	○	○
• Invitation methods do not confuse the child or muddle the message.	○	○	○	○	○
• _____	○	○	○	○	○

8. Children have regular opportunities to trust in Christ.

	1	2	3	4	5
• Evangelism of children is a priority of the church leadership.	○	○	○	○	○
• Parents receive training about how to lead their own children to Christ.	○	○	○	○	○
• Allocation of church resources reflects a recognition of the fruitfulness of evangelizing children.	○	○	○	○	○
• The church sees much fruit in children trusting in Christ as their Savior.	○	○	○	○	○
• _____	○	○	○	○	○

* 1—Always true; 2—True most of the time; 3—Sometimes true; 4—Rarely true; 5—Never true.

Notes

1. The ones in this book, of course.
2. Want a copy? Visit www.rorheiminstitute.org or www.gospellight.com to download the matrix.

Rock-Solid Standards for Children's Ministry

Standard 1:
Ministering to children is a high priority.

Standard 2:
The responsibility for children's ministry first belongs to parents.

Standard 3:
Scripture is the foundation of our content; relevance follows.

Standard 4:
Spiritual training of children is the core lifestyle of the home.

Standard 5:
Every child is safe and loved at all times.

Standard 6:
Children serve God as soon as they are ready.

Standard 7:
**Children's workers communicate the gospel
with clarity and urgency.**

Standard 8:
Children have regular opportunities to trust in Christ.

Scripture Index